Emerging Proud Press
The Enterprise Centre
Norwich  NR4 7TJ
United Kingdom

ISBN: 978-1-9160860-0-5
www.EmergingProud.com

**KindaPR UD**
Stories of Hope & Transformation

## DEDICATION

This book is dedicated to all those whose lives are
anything but ordinary.
May you find your gifts, use them well, and shine
unapologetically bright.
You are here to do amazing things.

**"And the day came when the risk to
remain tight in a bud was more painful
than the risk it took to blossom."**
**Anais Nin**

*The Kindaproud pocket books are a wonderful resource, full of amazing stories of transformation. I was deeply moved and inspired by reading them.*

Dr. Steve Taylor, author of
*The Leap* and *Spiritual Science.*

# More praise for Kinda Proud

*Having come across Kinda Proud was like discovering a beautiful flower emerging from the compost pile of contemporary human society. The often painfully-earned wisdom shared by the individuals within this book offers crucial guidance to those individuals going through such challenging crises themselves. But even more than this, I believe that the wisdom contained within this book conveys a message for all of us—to each of us individually as well as to all of us collectively as a human society entering enormously challenging times: Even within the midst of great confusion, despair and turmoil, we can trust that intrinsic within the very nature of our beings lie the seeds of profound healing and transformation. We only need to find the courage to open our eyes and our hearts to the suffering and the joy within and around us, as the brave souls in this book have so nobly demonstrated.*

Paris Williams, PhD, Clinical Psychologist, Director of *The Centre for Nonviolence and Conscious Living* <u>cncl.info</u>, and author of *Rethinking Madness* <u>rethinkingmadness.com</u>

*These stories will inspire and uplift you. They will help you to see that you are not alone, that you too can come through your darkest hour. From childhood illness to suppressed family secrets, the stories represent the full range of traumatic, painful life experiences. But the message is one of hope; the triggers for crisis are also the source of awakening, of shifting to a new level of consciousness.*

*Read about the contributors' journeys and prepare to embark on the healing journey of a lifetime, your lifetime.*

Catherine G. Lucas, Founder, UK Spiritual Crisis Network, author of *In Case of Spiritual Emergency: Moving Successfully Through Your Awakening* and other books on healing through crisis. Her latest is *Life Crisis: the Mindful Way.*

*This series of books demonstrates the importance of understanding why we must begin to treat all people with exceptional human experiences, mystical experiences, depression, and other non-ordinary states with respectful curiosity about the potential transformational benefits they may offer the experiencers. Transformation and healing is delayed by professionals who refuse to listen to their clients and patients. Let these books be your guide on the questions to ask.*

Elizabeth J. Sabet, PCC, ACLSC, CBC President of the American Center for the Integration of Spiritually Transformative Experiences https://aciste.org

*Each of these shared stories make captivating reading, whether you are new to NOTEs or are familiar with the breadth and depth possible within the human experience.*

*I am excited to see this collection. I am pleased that more and more people around the world are sharing their accounts so that we recognise and embrace the frequency with which they are occurring. We can allow our understanding of the range of 'normal' to include these phenomena. I thank each and every person waking up amongst us, for their bravery and courage, through troubling and ecstatic times, through the nightmare and the bliss, through taboo and isolation.*

*Out of all the messages I have seen to be crucial when supporting those in distress, my favourite is that each of us are "not alone". Thank you to the Emerging Proud campaign, through these Kinda Proud books, for providing clear evidence of this! There is a growing tribe of experiencers. We can support each other on many levels. Enjoy!*

Ali Chapman, ISEN (International Spiritual Emergence Network Core Team)
http://www.spiritualemergencenetwork.org

*Too many talented individuals have literally been 'hexed' into believing they have a permanent pathological brain condition by a culture and mental health system that does not understand the growth potential of a psychological crisis or the potential pathways to recovery.*

*During the production and distribution of our film CRAZYWISE I have heard from hundreds of individuals who have successfully navigated a severe mental emotional crisis. Many had to take the often disorienting and frightening journey into extra ordinary states of consciousness without any help or guidance. (In fact, CRAZYWISE has now been translated into 16 languages voluntarily by several of these individuals which has allowed it to be seen in 54 countries.)*
*I have often thought of what we can do to change the common consensus about a psychological crisis from a*

*pathology to an opportunity. How do we support those in crisis and encourage more of those who have navigated a crisis to share their journeys of transformation and come out from under the cultural cloud of stigma and shame to share their process?*

**By making these initiatory but difficult experiences a cause for pride and celebration of strength and courage - this remarkable book series does just that!**

Phil Borges, Co-Producer/Director CRAZYWISE (www.crazywisefilm.com)

## Power of the Collective

It is not only those who achieve
what we would see as great things
but the number of us who, each day,
do something small from our hearts
who will have the biggest effect
on the way the world is.

By Ambriel

# Contents

# About KindaProud

## Our KindaProud Pocket Book series
## Ethos and Message

Why do we need 'KindaProud' Pocket Books of Hope and Transformation? There is a rising epidemic of mental health problems in our society, and alongside it a pervasive negative prognosis message that goes out to those who are struggling emotionally. It's our shared belief, due to our personal experiences, that one of the most important elements of getting back on a road to recovery (and ultimately transformation) is to normalise these experiences and to hear personal stories of HOPE from those who have been there before and not just survived, but thrived.

Each Pocket Book has its own KindaProud Rep; a Peer who has personal experience of 'coming through' the theme of that specific book. These are the first 4 books currently in the series: -

- #Emerging Proud through NOTEs (Non-Ordinary Transcendent Experiences)
- #Emerging Proud through Disordered Eating, Poor Body Image and Low Self- Esteem
- #Emerging Proud through Suicide
- #Emerging Proud through Trauma and Abuse

# What are the main Aims and Objectives of the KindaProud Pocket Book series?

- To relieve people of the distress associated with transformational crises by offering authentic examples of personal stories and resources to engender hope and initiate recovery.

- To decrease stigma, improve wellbeing and influence the saving of lives by providing a more compassionate and positive conceptual framework for emotional distress.

- To use the profits from book sales to continue to distribute free books, and hence messages of HOPE, to mental health facilities, and those in need, all around the world.

All of the stories in this book have been kindly donated by Peers who have personally experienced this specific theme of distress and 'emerged transformed'; dedicated to giving hope that there is light at the end of the tunnel to others who may still be suffering. This book series is totally not-for-profit, was seed-funded by *The Missing Kind charity*, and continues to be supported voluntarily through the endless dedication of each Peer Rep, our Ambassador and Publisher Sean Patrick of *That Guy's House* who supported us to set up #Emerging Proud Press, and Jenna Gould, our 'PR Guru' of *Media Jems*.

## Meet Sean our Publisher and Ambassador!

I guess you could say that I was a typical Millennial/ Gen Y kind of guy. I lived life on the 'ordinary' path; going from High School to College to University to my first job in the City. Embracing all of the joys of young professional city life (like I'd seen so much on TV growing up), however, having the curse of also knowing that my life needed to have meaning and without it I was doomed. And so right on time, feelings of anxiety and depression became present in my early 20s, with social anxiety leading on to more serious depression.

Like many people I didn't know where I fitted into the world, and despite having the things I was 'supposed to', I felt unhappy, anxious and unfulfilled. I felt like I was on a treadmill and scared by the world.

My 'crisis point' hit when I started to experience severe panic attacks at 22 years old. It was then that I had no option but to admit I had problems that at that time I couldn't rationalise with my own intellect or understanding. In other words, I was having a mental health crisis.

I started by reading books, gaining a better understanding of my own mind, and ultimately to a more spiritual outlook on life through daily meditation and adopting spiritual beliefs. I had read these books from being 15 so it was 'old hat' for me, however, a 22 year old having a crisis could engage with them with much more desperation than a 15 year old wanting to be his best self.

After accepting an expat job in Hong Kong and spending half a year away from my 'ordinary life', I had the chance to recalibrate, explore meditation and mindfulness, and let go of damaging old patterns and beliefs.

I turned my life upside down.

On returning home, I set up a blog called *That Guy Who Loves The Universe* and began to share ideas about spirituality and positive mental health with my following, which grew to over 15,000 people. I began to speak at conferences and wellness events all over the world and released an Amazon bestseller in July 2016.

My mess latterly became my message.

In 2017, I developed my own wellness company, *That Guy's House*, with a main focus on wellness books and mental health projects.

After meeting Katie, the project's Founder, via a synchronistic introduction by our #Emerging Proud through Suicide book Rep, Kelly, and finding out more about the #Emerging Proud campaign, Katie and I both knew that bringing our personal experiences and skills together to launch the KindaProud series of Pocket Books would be the perfect collaboration.

# Meet the Project's Founder

*My name is Katie Mottram and I'm the Founder of the #Emerging Proud campaign, through which the KindaProud book series has been birthed. #Emerging Proud is a grassroots social movement aimed at: 'Re-framing mental distress as a catalyst for positive transformation'; providing a platform for people who have 'emerged transformed' through a personal crisis and feel called to share their story and give hope to others. By no means does this mean the end of our personal journey, but rather that we now choose to view life's challenges more as growth opportunities as opposed to experiences set out to destroy us.*

I was called to start this movement due to finding that re-framing my own crisis as a transformational growth process (which still continues!), and hearing the experiences of others, was the thing that helped me to connect with my authentic Self and start to live the life I was born to live.

When I experienced a personal crisis in 2008, what I needed was to know that I wasn't alone in my experiences, that what I was going through was 'normal', and a message of HOPE, that all would be okay, not that there was anything 'wrong' with me. I needed to connect with others who had been through similar challenges and were able to walk alongside me whilst I found my own way out of the darkness.

In the last decade, it has been through my own research; looking at more empowering ways of understanding what happened to me, my reactions to it, and how to go about self-healing, in addition to connecting with my amazing peers and listening to their stories, that has really set me on my own path of healing. This feels like the complete opposite of what I had been told was helpful whilst working within mental health services for 15 years previously. Hence my passion to provide others with some of the tools that helped me not only to survive, but to thrive and love life.

You can read my full story in my own book, 'Mend the Gap: A transformative journey from deep despair to spiritual awakening', which I published in 2014.
I truly hope that this book, and the others in the 'Pocket Books of Hope and Transformation' series,

inspires and supports you in your own evolutionary journey...

And, remember to do what Nicole suggests; let that light you hold deep inside shine unapologetically bright!

Find out more about the campaign and what we're up to at: www.emergingproud.com

# Meet our Peer Pocket Book Rep,
# Dr Nicole Gruel

*Nicole Gruel is Kinda Proud, and so she should be! She's emerging as a world-leading Coach on NOTEs, due to her personal experience igniting a passion in her which led to her researching the transformational power of NOTEs for her doctoral study.*

*We couldn't be prouder to have Nicole as one of our KindaProud Pocket Books of Hope and Transformation Reps and are so grateful for her support of the project. Here she gives you an insight into her personal story that led to her passion for this work...*

A NOTE (non-ordinary transcendent experience) is a rare and unfamiliar event that takes us beyond our regular understanding of ourselves and the world. The term was coined by the late transpersonal psychologist William Braud as a way of bringing together the three fields of transpersonal psychology, exceptional human experiences, and psychical experiences.

There are hundreds of experiences that fit under the grand NOTEs umbrella, including spiritual awakening, near-death experience, out-of-body experience, peak experience, and any other extraordinary experience that seems to defy the laws of reality as we knew it until that moment. Even falling in love and big dreams can be considered NOTEs as they tend to alter our sense of time, place, and way of being in the world. These experiences are often forever life-altering.

Today, reports of NOTEs are on the rise. This is due to a potent blend of increased access to spiritual development tools and teachings, better life-saving technologies, planetary crises prompting personal crises, growing interest in hacking human potential, a revival in psychedelics, and the ability as a species to share information globally and instantly in ways we've never been able to do before.

I first came across the term NOTEs whilst researching for my doctoral dissertation. The term drew me in as it captured the vastness of what I understood these experiences to be in a way that was relatively neutral. I also like the metaphor of notes, like poignant music that punctuates important moments in life, or wine that leaves a lingering and subtle aftertaste.

My first NOTE I recall happened when I was a teenager, whilst white-water rafting in New Zealand. It was a glorious day and a friend and I set out on a river full of rapids with two guides. We had such a great time that we decided to do it again and raced back up the mountain so we could re-enter the river. The second time, however, the skies had turned grey, the atmosphere was somehow heavy, and as we got to the largest waterfall (a 10 meter/33-foot drop), our raft flipped over and I fell out. I opened my arms to swim but that only pushed me deeper under the gushing waterfall. In an instant, the water around me was black and I didn't know which way was up or down. I didn't know where to swim and there was no point trying. I desperately wanted to breathe and after a moment of sheer panic came absolute calm and stillness.

Deep down in the blackness of the water, a brilliant horizon of light opened before me. If you've ever seen the movie "Ghost", it was a lot like that moment Sam and Molly are reunited. Walking toward me from the horizon of light was my (then living) grandmother and (then deceased) pet dog. As a young teenager I thought this was a bit curious and wondered what they were doing there. It all felt lovely, very peaceful, and so natural.

Then, a strong and clear male voice from behind my shoulder said, "Nicole, don't forget to breathe". And, just like that, the memory returned of the safety briefing we'd received that morning should we fall out of the raft, and I curled up into a ball as taught so that I'd rise to the surface like a cork. It worked, and soon enough the water changed to dark green, then light green, then white, and I surfaced to breathe. I never thought too much of this experience and the impact it may have had until later in my 20s. For now, I was simply relieved to still be alive.

Within the next 6 months, I lost my father and two other family members, all in separate sudden incidents, in countries far away, and without the chance to say goodbye. I later came to call this chapter of my life "initiation through death". As recognized in shamanic traditions, once having passed through such a gateway, life is never to be the same. Indeed, this was my rather brutal introduction to 'That which is beyond ordinary life'.

Throughout my 20s, I continued to be drawn to anything related to personal and spiritual growth and development. I read up on and tasted various traditions and wisdom paths in a quest to understand the core of me and what I am to do on this planet. I was thirsty for experiences that satisfied a sense of meaning and purpose. I travelled widely the outer worlds and inner worlds. I was blessed to have many other NOTEs that helped connect and acquaint me with the non-ordinary. Though not always pleasant experiences, I came to better understand the extraordinariness that we as humans can access and the forces we can work with to bring about healing, change, transformation, and creative genius.

As I turned 30 I was to have another life-changing NOTE; one that gave me a direct experience to the eternal core of my being. As they say, be careful what you ask for! It occurred spontaneously (though one could argue that these kinds of things are never really spontaneous, rather, one is ripe for a NOTE to occur). Over 3 days, a fever took over and I experienced movement between ordinary and altered states of consciousness. I had not taken any substances, though I now had over a decade of conscious practice of opening experiences to help me understand and trust what was happening. Although my family requested I go to the hospital for my ongoing high fever, I knew something important was happening and wanted to ride it through, promising to go to the hospital if really need be.

In a nutshell, those three days were like the peeling of an onion, where every single layer was part of my identity. The peeling continued until, towards the end of the three days, there was nothing left but a pinprick of light. I knew in that moment that incy-wincy pinprick was 'All that I am'. Nothing more, nothing less. Everything beyond that, any layer of the onion, was a construction I could co-create in this grand game of life on planet earth. And so it has been since.

There have been other NOTEs since then, which is a common experience for NOTErs. Rather than those profound life experiences that happen and fade over time, NOTEs are a special kind that seem to do the opposite. They often snowball over the years. In any case, their sacredness and specialness rarely leaves the experiencer.

And so, today, this is why I am devoted to working with other NOTErs to make the most of their experiences. We dive deep to understand the experience(s), their wisdom, process whatever needs processing, integrate the pieces that seek resolution in the magnificent wholeness of our being, and then take practical actions toward creating the life that most deeply calls them. I am of the belief that the more we do this, the more our genius naturally shines through, and the more we can each get on with whatever it is we're here on planet earth to do.

I hold the vision that one day NOTEs will be a term as common as 'flow', 'peak', or 'yoga'. That what we today consider extraordinary will be accepted and celebrated as an important capacity of our natural human being-ness. Like Maslow once dreamed, I too dream of a time when we hold "classes in miraculousness". I look forward to the day when care is truly holistic and those who need the services of professionals will be met with specialists of the body, mind AND spirit. Then, we may truly start to see what we are capable of as a species and properly address the problems we face on this planet.

*Dr. Nicole Gruel is passionate about creating spiritual health and life wealth for all. As an author, speaker, samurai descendent and transformational coach, she helps people craft the life they most deeply desire with warrior focus. She has spent over two decades exploring human potential and how ordinary people make the most* of extraordinary experiences to become their best as lovers, leaders, and human Beings. Her latest book, "The Power of NOTEs: how non-ordinary transcendent experiences transform the way we live, love, and lead" was published in 2018.

You can find out more about Nicole at: _www. drnicolegruel_.com.

**Altazar's life transformed the moment he decided he could no longer fit himself into the boxes of our 'cultural matrix'**

*Pretty much anyone who has #Emerged Proud to date can relate to Altazar's words of wisdom here:*

*"Who I was being had no relevance to my true self. My identity was in meltdown. And I knew this crisis had been brewing for a long time...I decided that I had to be true to myself, whatever that looked like, or die in the process."*

*It's usually the meaning we find within the crisis that points us in the direction of our purpose. We have to succumb to the emotions we've been repressing, often for years, for the healing journey to begin. However, calming the Ego enough to let go and trust this necessary fall is not at all an easy thing to do, as Altazar recounts through his story...*

I've never been diagnosed with any mental disorder. Probably because, somehow, I had the nous to stay out of the medical system. Nevertheless, I believe my experience would today be classified as a mental/emotional breakdown and burnout. I was walking down the street having arguments with myself – out loud, for Christ's sake!

When I realised this, I got very scared. I certainly did not want it on my medical records jeopardising future employment prospects, loading insurance premiums or producing any other unnecessary challenges in my life.

I was 37 years old, working as an electrical design engineer in a well-paid, very rational, male-dominated industry. However, that industry was in deep recession and my job would soon disappear with no hope of finding anything similar. My marriage was falling apart. I was completely shut down emotionally. My life was a mess. I was certainly depressed. I was toxic to be around.

Looking back now it's obvious that I was going through a major spiritual awakening. I'd been living my life inside the boxes prescribed by convention. Outwardly, I looked successful, but I hated myself. Those boxes I'd put myself in never did fit me and they'd led me to be very fragmented. I was different people for different aspects of my life, and inauthentic in virtually all of them.

Who I was being had no relevance to my true self. My identity was in meltdown. And I knew this crisis had been brewing for a long time.

I needed to sort myself out. I had no idea how, but I decided that I had to be true to myself, whatever that looked like, or die in the process. If I couldn't find some real meaning to my existence and integrate that into the way I lived I did not want to be here.

By chance, I was in the old St Pancras library one day in my lunchtime and picked up a flyer for a ten-week course about stress and burnout. I read it and ticked all the boxes twice over. It was like someone had left it there especially for me. I signed up immediately. To the person I was then, it was all weird. There were some basic psychological exercises (Transactional Analysis), story-telling, role-playing, reflexology, massage and meditation. It was the meditation that saved me.

We were taught a version of the Buddhist Metta Bhavana (loving kindness) practice. It saved my life. I embraced it wholeheartedly, as if something in me remembered it from another existence.

My marriage collapsed; my job disappeared. It took

about two years to regain some sense of equilibrium after that.

I practised my meditation daily, although I did nothing else metaphysical for about five years. But I was changing.

I found a job that I could manage easily, and I enrolled in a part-time degree course at what is now Middlesex University, reading English. I wanted to take a completely different direction. That was where the five years went.

Initially the degree was something to keep me busy and at home, as my fourteen-year-old son chose to live with me instead of his mother. But I evolved; I did well, and I got interested in psychoanalytic literary criticism – something most other students avoided like the plague. As I got deeper into how we make meaning of things I started to see the meanings I'd made up about my own existence. My interpretations of my experiences had plainly accumulated into a perception of myself and life in general that just had to implode at some point. I was seeing why I'd made such a mess of my life. Coupled with the meditation practice this enabled me to accept and forgive myself for much of the mess I'd created.

I graduated with a good first-class honours that allowed me to be accepted directly onto a PhD programme without taking an interim master's degree. I was researching how we make sense of ourselves through linguistic structures. Ultimately, this was analysing my own process through close examination of the way I made meaning out of various texts, and how I mapped that onto the reality of my life.

And just as I was getting into my PhD I got a shock. What I now know as my healing channels opened spontaneously in meditation. I had no reference points for this, and again I was scared. My body tingled with energy from head to toe. I could visualise it, and turn it on and off.

At this time I was also in a new relationship, with someone who had a passing interest in spirituality. I didn't tell my partner about my experience for a few days; when I did she encouraged me to explore the realm of spiritual healing. I had nothing to lose, so that was the beginning of a sojourn through New Age spirituality that lasted several years.

It was a lot of fun and sometimes very scary. I found the territory populated with a mixture of sincerity and superficiality, integrity and exploitation. It was a minefield.

There was LOADS of emotional work: buckets full of tears and rage. There was more than one experience of what is known generically as the dark night of the soul, which is more accurately the mind going into a flat spin because nothing it knows can cope with the fractures in its sense of reality.

But I was on a path. There was enough consistency in my spiritual adventures to keep me engaged.

I looked at various forms of energy healing, in an attempt to give myself some kind of label, and I learned a great deal from all of them. The most commonly recognised form I learned was Reiki, which I actually taught for four years. But, I've been consistently driven to find my own way.

As a child I could remember being a man in another life – I still can; I saw things – beings, entities that "weren't there" according to my parents – I still do. However, I went into denial about my inherent spiritual nature for nearly thirty years because a difficult experience with religion at the age of ten turned me against anything religious, and by implication spiritual.

Since my initial episode of mental instability, I've gradually been better able to join the dots of my life into a coherent picture. That picture is not static, which is also a challenge to a mind that craves stability, but it gets clearer all the time. What is crystal clear is that there are few reliable reference points in our culture for the process of spiritual awakening. Hearing voices and seeing visions may not book your ticket to the funny farm, but it will qualify you for some addictive medication to slug your sensitivity – if you tell the wrong people.

These days I support others as they awaken to their spiritual nature. I help them to learn to trust themselves, their intuition and their magic, and find their way to engage with what I call their Spiritual Intelligence. The 37-year-old electrical engineer I was would have said you were mad, had you told him this was where he was headed.

*The mainstream cultural matrix functions as a control device to keep us afraid of ourselves, calling our inherent magic "madness". You embody its inherent psychosis if you go along with it.*

*Find out more about Altazar's work at:*
*www.altazarrossiter.com*

"Re-examine all you have been told
in school or church or in any book,
Dismiss whatever insults your own soul"

Walt Whitman's Preface to Leaves of Grass
(1885 edition)

**Linda describes how her journey through confusion and chaos led to her finding the truth about who she is, and what gifts she has to offer the world as a result**

*Linda's story is a special one for me (Katie, #Emerging Proud Founder) to share, as Linda was one of the few people who offered me a non-judgemental safe space to work through my own crisis in 2012. We travelled the unfolding of our journeys alongside each other, often mirroring, and triggering, each other to growth...*

*As Linda explains, her repressed trauma catalysed a spiritual awakening for her, and without a prior context for that, the chaos that ensued caused instability, as it does for many who experience a spontaneous awakening.*

*Today, 7 years on, Linda is bringing her individual passion for providing deep listening that emerged from her crisis into both her own life's mission and a joint project that we are evolving together; the transformational opportunities of crisis indeed! Hear Linda's journey through her own words...*

As the dowsing rod spun faster and faster above my head, I felt a release in my body and a teardrop trickle down my cheek.

Confused by my emotional response, I asked what was happening...

The course leader explained that I was probably feeling the relief of freely accessing my innate feminine gift of connecting with earth energy. She explained that, for generations, we have repressed our innate sensory, intuitive and supernatural gifts, to protect ourselves from the risk of being drowned or burnt at the stake, as these gifts were associated with witchery. Now it is 'safe' to be who we really are, without the risks of the past: the release I felt was ancestral, as well as personal.

There had been no room in my life for drama, or the non-ordinary and I had no context in my upbringing for the spiritual, supernatural or transcendental. My 45 years had been happy, stable and sweet. In early 2011, I began to feel increasingly highly sensitive and euphoric and this coincided with a new awareness of synchronicity and receiving messages from vivid dreams with symbols of sacred geometry. As well as feeling more emotional, I also felt frequent blissful moments as though cradled in a silky wrap of unconditional love and floating on a cloud of cotton wool. The euphoria continued intermittently for around four months.

More extreme, was having a vision (or hallucination?) of light emanating from the soil. I had a 'knowing' that the mirror-like points of light were some kind of message, though it must have been for my subconscious as I had no idea what the message was. Although I felt completely comfortable during the experience, I did feel concerned the following morning when I described the event out loud.

A few times over those months, I found myself emerging from spontaneous, trance-like states with a disparate view of the world: the revelations were liberating, and I became evangelical (and probably very annoying) about what I had 'seen' and now 'knew' to be true. Although many of these revelations have since become mainstream, my values changing 180 degrees overnight caused chaos in my life and for my family.

We had no context for my experiences and it was assumed that my 'instability' was at best a mid-life crisis and at worst a psychotic breakdown and imbalance of chemicals in my brain. Feeling misunderstood, alone and alienated from everyone who had ever known and loved me, it was a relief to meet someone who shared their similar anomalous experiences and so fully accepted and understood what I was experiencing.

I was only fleetingly aware of the internal split I was feeling and, at one point, when feeling desperately confused and alienated, I fell to my knees and prayed for the first time in my life... and within 15 minutes I had received an answer - a direct experience of 'God' which, considering my atheist upbringing, was unacceptable! I was buoyed up by visions of angels radiating their healing light to protect my family... chaos ensued...!

Within a few months, the gravity of the pain and shock I'd passed on to my family began to pierce my heart and I spiralled into despair. Amidst my vulnerability, I made it my mission to understand exactly what had happened to me mentally, emotionally, psychologically and spiritually. I embarked on a journey and immersed myself in exploration, research and study; including questioning and listening to peers. This gave me good understanding of the nature of my spiritual awakening, experiences and life crisis, as well as the healing processes that followed...

In February 2011, I was shocked at being introduced to my half-brother at a family party. He had been kept a secret from us. I felt gushing compassion for him, as he had not known the wonderful Dad my late father was. I welcomed him into our family. A series of revelations about my birth family followed and I tried to understand my parents' decisions. Although I was dealing with my anger consciously and moving towards forgiveness, something deep within my psychological foundation had shifted and it was as though, as the truth about my family was revealed, so too was the truth about the world and, in time, the truth about who I am.

It is only in retrospect that I realise, that in hearing the truth around my father, I'd felt a trauma and it had triggered a deep break in my psyche. I had indeed lost much of my rational capacity: it was as though my left brain took a break and my energy flooded my right brain. Maybe, just as the truth about my family had been repressed, parts of who I am had been repressed and the revelations gave an opening and permission for those repressed parts of my psyche to be liberated, in an explosion of unconscious chaos, as I suddenly became sensitive, tuned in and alive with my new intuitive gifts and emotional state: contrasting with the fairly quiet, logical, rational and composed wife and mother, I had been.

There are maybe two reasons that I managed to hold on to my sanity through these months: -

1. I had a strong solid foundation - for 45 years before the shock, I had lived a stable and happy life

2. Intuitively, I found a group of people who listened to me with skill and who validated and normalised my experiences as they shared their similar experiences. Gaining courage to share more and hearing myself, helped me make sense of my story. I began to accept myself and realise the strength and gifts I'd gained from my crisis.

My confidence grew and, gradually, I clawed back my rational capacity and the spirals of healing, rebalancing and integration continue…

**Making sense of my challenges in a way that contributes to others feeling heard and understood, to enhance their wellbeing, is an important part of my journey.**

Initially, I felt compelled to offer the same support I'd received and so facilitated a peer support group. Katie had encouraged me to start the group through a vision she'd had! We all felt the relief each week of having a safe space to share our experiences that we couldn't comfortably share with family, colleagues or other friends. The bonds we made over those two years were strong and we are still connected now.

I developed my 'KindaListening' project as a training programme to enhance connection and empower people to resource themselves and each other; by developing stronger skills in deeper listening and empowering conversation. Feeling heard helps!

KindaListening is proving to be a strong 'revolutionary' foundation for communication that empowers self-awareness and authentic, conscious expression; enabling creating a safe space for others to share. As such, it has become a key foundational training for Peer Group Facilitation. This was initially for the Emerging Kind Peer Group Facilitator training, inspired by Katie's Emerging Proud event in 2017, and then for our Support Source Community Sharing

Circles Facilitator training which was Big Lottery funded. We are now rippling out the benefits of being heard to sustain wellbeing within organisations.

**Magic!**

*To find out more about what Linda's training offers, go to:*

*www.KindaListening.org / www.LindaAllen.net*

**It took a brush with death for Erica to truly embrace her life and her true Self**

*Erica McKenzie, a registered nurse, was able to find and love her authentic Self only catalysed through a crisis, that led to an NDE (near-death experience), which she now sees as a blessing. Erica's words will resonate with many:*

*"I've spent my entire life trying to be everything to everyone, and in the process, I lost myself."*

*Through the messages received during her transcendent state of consciousness, she discovered that it was going within, listening to our intuition and surrendering to 'God' (which others term, Source or the Divine /*

*the Universe), is the only answer we need to find our purpose in life. That purpose is to be true to ourselves, for each one of us has a unique gift to offer the world.*

*Here Erica recounts her incredible brush with death that led her in and out of a psychiatric unit...*

Many of us feel lost and struggle to find direction and purpose in life. In my case, one of the most challenging things I was faced with learning was to love my unique self, just as God made me. This challenge was one that stuck with me my entire childhood and accompanied me into adulthood. I spent too many years wanting others to accept me and was convinced that changing myself to fit in with whomever I was around at the time, was the answer. This behavior sent me down a path where I made several poor choices which included a twelve-year battle with bulimia and a drug problem that ultimately led to my death...

That fateful day in 2002, I had a near-death experience (NDE). My NDE was the point of my awakening, which led to my transformation. My experience taught me so many lessons but one of the most important things I learned was that: "Your uniqueness is your value and your value is your contribution on this Earthly Journey." I quickly came to appreciate the significance of this knowledge and, for the first time in my human existence, I finally understood: My uniqueness is my value because it holds my unique blueprint and unique gifts that serve to truly fulfil my life's purpose.

The mind is a powerful thing, and yet it fails in comparison to the knowledge found within our spiritual hearts. That knowledge is divine power. If we choose, we can unlock the answers by turning within and reconnecting to our creator through our hearts. I discovered that it is through this connection that I remember who I am, and it is through this connection that I am able to grow and nurture unconditional love for myself. This unconditional love is the key to ignite the power within. When we seek that power within, we gain the knowledge needed to help us through every life experience, and as we step into our power we reveal our blueprint and gifts.

We each have unique God-given gifts. To fully achieve their potential, we must use these gifts in conjunction with each other. It's only when we come to the table with our unique selves - whether it's the business table, the relationship table, or the dinner table - that we empower each other and can go on to do great things.

As I realized all of this, then it happened. In the winter of 2002, I surrendered and, in doing so, I knew this meant that I could no longer look to others for my value and wonder what people think about me. I had to refuse to let those feelings define me. I may not have all the answers, but I don't have to look to others for approval, and having feelings of uncertainty is actually… OK. I can acknowledge those feelings now, using them as tools that help me trust there is nothing I can't get through because I see things differently now. I have faith that God is at work in my life, and He has the answers, so I don't have to have them.

My purpose is to learn. My mission is to serve. My heart is to love. My boss is God and my work is to BE ME.

It was easy to accept this challenge when I was in Heaven with God. So, armed with this new Divine knowledge, I returned from my NDE determined to share my story in the hope it would help to create needed healing and awakening in others who were hurting.

When I regained consciousness, I found myself in a hospital bed and didn't know how much time had passed. I was desperately trying to make sense of my trip to Heaven when a doctor walked into my room and asked me how I was. I remember being flooded with a sense of urgency to share my NDE with him. As the words came flying out of my mouth, I began to sense his disbelief and concern for my mental health. Without a word, he quietly left the room and returned several hours later. At this time my NDE, and my experience with God, was dismissed - labeled a delusion and replaced with a medical diagnosis of late onset bipolar disorder. What followed next was a trip to the psychiatric ward against my will.

Overcome with memories from nursing school, I remembered the time I had on the psych ward as a nursing student. It was one of the more difficult things I'd done. It seemed like the patients there were forgotten people. My instructor had said it was important to appear attentive and to act as if you were listening. "Mental health care provides people the opportunity to lead a normal life like everyone else, and these people are not normal," she stated.

She also said not to believe what the patients were saying because they were not speaking truth, but merely attempting to manipulate. I knew it was wrong in nursing school and didn't understand how some people could be so cruel. I was told the patients were crazy, yet several of them appeared to have the ability to communicate with something we couldn't see. I felt that many of them were medicated because of it. It was horrible. I'd grown up believing that the purpose of medicine was to heal the sick, not to turn people into something they were not.

Here I was, years later, in the exact same position as some of those patients, being dismissed and medicated because I had an experience – a crisis the doctor couldn't explain. Call sharing my NDE crazy if you must – you won't hear me challenge it. But what did being crazy really mean? And did it constitute a solution if the cure came in the form of a pill? Maybe I was just broken and lost, or maybe I was displaying acute mental distress that was evolving into a positive healing transformation.

I realized through my own experience that those patients needed to be heard by an educated, empathetic and caring staff. I couldn't help but feel the majority of the drugs administered to many of these patients acted as a Band-Aid, only able to reduce or mask the symptoms temporarily, if they were therapeutic at all. I sensed the drugs affected the ability of several of the patients to think clearly. Even more terrifying, I sensed the drugs were changing those people, and I'm certain in some cases they blocked communication to God.

It was a crash course in mental health care, starting with my perceived "crazy behavior and delusions." Everything that happened to me up until the day I died, including my trip to Heaven, Hell and the psych ward, was preparing me to help myself and others. That help would include: educating the medical community that near-death experiences, the presence of God and our ability to connect with our Creator within them, should be seen as a miracle, not a medical issue. And that, in fact, these miracles would provide great healing.

At the same time, I knew that before I could begin to fix the system and help others, I had to heal myself. I was broken, so it was going to be hard work because it was a constant battle between healing and changing me. I understood these to be two completely different approaches, and according to everything I had just learned in Heaven, it was more evident to me than ever that the answer wasn't to change me. Even if the staff had the best intentions for restoring my health, it was clear that their approach was going to lead to changing, not healing, me. I understood for many that the word 'change' had taken on a meaning that had the potential to improve or destroy the human condition. And yet there was no doubt in my mind that all the obstacles I had been through and the roadblocks that were ahead were no match for the knowledge I gained in Heaven. I knew that with God all things were possible.

I can't imagine the countless individuals who have experienced spiritual events and have been medicated and dismissed because of it. When does communicating with the unseen or spiritual realm validate a diagnosis of psychosis? It appears society, and especially the medical community, is in dire need of education on NDEs from a spiritual level. The effect of doing so would have the potential to increase their receptiveness and support of their patients' experiences.

I've spent my entire life trying to be everything to everyone and in the process, I lost myself. I have loved many but I couldn't love myself. I didn't think I was good enough or deserving of that self-love, and I felt selfish for wanting it. Now I see that way of thinking, and engaging in toxic behaviors, changed me and led me in the opposite direction from becoming a self-advocate and completing my earthly mission.

My NDE has not changed my life – it has GIVEN me life, by opening my eyes to see my value. It has reawakened me to the real Erica, the little child who was in touch with God and His gifts before I let fear in and started to stifle my feelings, doubt my intuition and drown out the voice of God in an effort to listen to others. So, armed with my knowledge and tools, I began the long and challenging road that would lead to healing, valuing my life, and becoming an advocate for myself and others.

"You matter.  You are important.
You are unique.
You are valuable.  And most of all,
You are loved!"

# Christina from Sydney, Australia, transformed her pain into her purpose via a journey to self-heal

*Christina's story, as unique to her as there are individuals on the planet, is so resonant of the collective voices who #Emerge Proud. Discovering profound meaning in our pain - light in the darkness - this is something that echoes throughout the reported learnings of all NOTEs experiencers and Empaths.*

*We couldn't agree more with Christina when she says: "As a 'healer' my job is to hold space, channeling energy to help you understand the 'why' in order for you to heal your wounds".*

*As Christina discovered, we can only heal ourselves when we make the decision to no longer be a victim to the challenges that life throws at us to help us grow…*

My name is Christina and my story goes something like this…

Proof that anything is possible if you believe.
I was born on an island called Cyprus and, at birth, both my hips were dislocated but the doctors missed it. It was not until I was four years old, thanks to a persistent and determined mother who knew there was something wrong, that they realised what had happened and why I was unable to walk.

The doctors told my mum that if I were to ever walk, she would have to take me to England for the surgery I needed, and urgently, or I would be in a wheelchair for the rest of my life. My mother took me to England for the surgery. They placed screws in both my hips and I spent six months in plaster from the chest to the toes. I still remember when they finally cut the plaster off and I was able to stand up for the very first time. The freedom to be able to move again after feeling suffocated and unable to move for so long was incredible.

A year later I returned to hospital for more surgery to take the screws out. I was encased in plaster once more. History was repeating itself. The surgery was a success on the left hip but not on the right hip. I was experiencing pain. The following year there was a war in my country and my family fled to Australia.

The pain continued and, at the age of twelve, my mum was told that I needed to have further surgery. It was decided that putting a screw in my hip would relieve the pain.

I spent my twelfth birthday in a hospital having my fifth surgery and was bedridden for six weeks, with my legs tied up in straps. This was followed by two months on crutches. During that hospital stay I saw my mum crying in the corridor next to my room and I made the conscious decision that I would never enter a hospital again or complain about the pain. The surgery was not a success. It only made the pain worse. It wasn't until years later that I discovered that they should never have put that screw in.

By my early twenties the pain had become unbearable at times. It felt like someone was stabbing me in the hip. The pain would shoot down my leg. It didn't help that I was studying to be a helicopter pilot. The vibrations of the helicopter irritated it even more. I decided to go to see a doctor as I loved flying. It was my escape from reality. I was told that the only way to alleviate the pain was to get a plastic hip. I was also told that the pain would get worse as I got older until I would be unable to walk.

That was the last time I saw a doctor. I had tried everything. I spent a small fortune on physiotherapists, healers, chiropractors, etc. but nothing really worked, not long-term anyway. I used to think that physical pain was far worse than emotional pain. At least with emotional pain you could cry yourself to sleep and have a rest.

None of this was helped by the fact that I am an Empath – something I didn't realise about myself until I went looking for answers. What that means is, I can feel other people's pain. I am very sensitive to the suffering on this planet. This, in turn, would make my own pain worse. There was a time when it became so bad that I began to think I was going mad. Certainly, growing up, I thought my sensitivity was a curse.

However, on my journey through this life I have come to see being an Empath as the great gift it is. I realised that it was up to me to heal my hip. My body, my responsibility. I refused to believe that I was sent to this world to suffer. I questioned what sort of "God" (I grew up in a Christian home) would create me in their image just to suffer, especially since I considered myself to be a "good" person.

In 2000, at the age of 32, I went backpacking around the world; not only to try and make sense of this existence, but also to find ways to heal myself. I was very fortunate to be invited to stay with medicine women in New Mexico and this was where I found my first genuine teacher, a Navaho. My healing journey began. I had always had a thing for native Indians, even as a little girl. I wanted to meet them, so this was a dream come true. It was an awakening. They helped me to remember who I am and to make peace with a world that seemed incredibly cruel and unjust.

As fate would have it, after my sojourn with these medicine women, I ended up in Guatemala, where I spent six months studying with three shamans who showed me ways to heal my body. To my surprise it worked! I was able to release the pain! So I continued to pursue more studies, spending more and more time with Indigenous medicine people and shamans. You can check out my journey on my website below.

This was the catalyst for my becoming a "healer". I say "healer" but it's not really a word I like to use, as only YOU can heal yourself. As a "healer" my job is to hold space, channeling energy to help you understand the "why" in order for you to heal your wounds. I share the tools that helped me heal my body physically, mentally and spiritually.

A word of caution; if you find a "healer" who promises to heal you, they are talking out of their ass, so run. Only YOU can heal yourself.

The mind is a powerful tool. If you don't believe you can heal it doesn't matter what anyone does, you won't heal because you have free will. Playing the victim does not serve. What you are going through is merely a lesson that you have chosen to experience. I learnt that you can use your experiences and wounds as the reason to be a victim and play the blaming game, or you can use them as an inspiration to become all that you can be and more. The choice is yours.

I am now 50 years old. My pain did not get worse. In fact, I am rarely in pain these days. I do not have a plastic hip and I've been able to trek through the Amazon, climb Machu Picchu, scale mountains and can walk for hours without pain. I actually feel better and am fitter now than I was in my 20s. The things we take for granted! To be able to walk and not be in pain is truly the most incredible gift. I am so grateful. As a child I thought I was being punished, that I had done something terribly wrong. Now I know that it was the greatest gift. My hips, my pain, were my inspiration to go out there and do all the things I dreamt of doing. Things I was told I could never do. To search for and find the answers and tools I needed to heal myself. Tools I now take great joy in sharing with others for use in their own healing.

**"Live every moment as if it's your last for tomorrow may never come."**

*Find Christina's website here: www.alkehela.com*

## Dr Mick Collins shares his experience of being a 'Wounded transformer'

*Although every account of a NOTE is unique to the individual, there are clear patterns that emerge through the stories shared, which seem to show how common themes of human struggle and survival connect us all at a soul level. Mick's deeply personal account is no exception. In fact, it clearly highlights the documented stages of a spiritual awakening: repression of struggles, trauma acting as a catalyst for change, repressed emotions surfacing for healing, growing conscious awareness, healing and transformation.*

*Knowing these stages are natural and don't last forever is helpful when we are mid crisis; that the only way out is indeed through...as Dr. Mick Collins beautifully explains, in realising that his paranoia was the result of his living decades of split-off trauma and rage. He was able to learn probably the most important lesson on the journey back to wholeness: that the Ego (shadow) is not something to push away or fight against, but embracing it is actually an integral part of the individuation process. Here Mick explains how that was for him in his own painful personal transformation journey...*

**Wounded Transformers**

In 1956 my teenage mother became pregnant and after I was born my grandmother decided it would be best if I were adopted. The separation from my mother was complex, compounded by the fact that she was denied the opportunity to say goodbye to me on the day I was taken away. This life-changing event happened when I was three months old. Adoption works out well for many people, but there are risk factors that can impact adopted children and adults.

Today, the psychosocial effects of adoption trauma are much better understood, particularly the various difficulties that can multiply as children are growing up, which can include anxiety, depression and identity confusion. In the worst cases, adoption trauma can result in dissociation, anti-social behaviour, sexual promiscuity, suicide and homicide. Studies in the US have shown that adoptees account for around *2% of the population, yet they are over-represented in mental health and criminal justice services.

Some of these risk factors overshadowed my life.

My adoptive parents were in the military, which meant we constantly moved home. As an only child I quickly learnt that friends and social connections were transient, and that education had no continuity or meaning due to the lack of a national curriculum. Consequently, my life was permeated with an existential sense of loneliness and rootlessness, which was compounded by the highly unusual fact that my adoptive mum and dad both lost their parents when they were children. As far as I know, they had no siblings. My adoptive parents were good people who did their very best for me, but they also had their own complexities.

Despite my unconventional family situation, life at home was relatively 'normal' and mostly non-eventful. However, at times the atmosphere became unpredictable and volatile, which also resulted in me experiencing double binds that were confusing and disorientating. I did not know which messages to trust, so I withdrew emotionally and became a people-pleaser. Yet deep down all was not well, as revealed in the nightly episodes of bed-wetting, which continued until I left home at seventeen. I also had a recurring paranoid fear that I would be hung for 'something' I did not do.

Throughout childhood I had very low expectations for my life. I left school at fifteen with no educational attainments and my first job was working on a building site as a labourer. It was not long before I started to go 'off the rails' and I appeared in court for the first time aged fifteen. It was a very troubling period of my life, which resulted in three further prosecutions for theft, threatening behaviour and possession of an offensive weapon.

An unexpected opportunity to change happened during a conversation with a kind police sergeant following my arrest for possession of an offensive weapon. He suggested I could do a lot better in life, and his non-judgemental attitude had a positive impact on me. I started reflecting on what I could do differently to turn my life around. When I appeared in court I was expecting a custodial sentence, but I spoke sincerely about wanting to join the army. Thankfully, I left court that day with a heavy fine, along with a deep resolve to try and change my attitudes and behaviours.

In 1974 I joined the infantry, which provided me with a real sense of containment, self-respect and belonging. My first posting was Northern Ireland, which taught me first-hand the impact of violence in a conflict zone. I left the forces after three and a half years. Between 1977-83 I travelled and worked around the world, which was liberating and a great cross-cultural education. Then, in 1983 I went for a two-day visit to see a friend who was living in a Tibetan Buddhist monastery and I ended up staying for three years. I immersed myself in Buddhist philosophy and meditation practice, whilst also learning ways to cultivate spiritual meaning in life.

It was during a short trip away from the monastery that I had a profound and life-changing numinous encounter, which happened whilst I was reciting mantras on a train. I suddenly experienced an overwhelming sense of love for everyone in the carriage. Everything was sacred and my whole body radiated bliss, which lasted for over two days. On the third day the experience gradually started to fade, and by the time I returned to the monastery I was starting to experience an extreme state of consciousness. I was overwhelmed by violent and murderous impulses, which catalysed a descent into a living hell that lasted for over two years.

A saving grace during this time was my having met an Indian psychologist and former mendicant, who had worked very closely with the great spiritual teacher, Jiddu Krishnamurti. He was well versed in Jungian and transpersonal psychology, as well as the world's mystical literature. He thought I was passing through a transformative spiritual experience, and his compassionate manner was literally life saving. I held tightly to his words, as it was all I had. In 1986 there was very little appreciation of such transformative processes in mainstream society; Stanislav Grof's book on spiritual emergency had not yet been published.

During my spiritual crisis I thought I was possessed by evil and on one occasion I came close to suicide. I was very troubled by the violence and murderousness within me, and I decided that I would rather end my own life than hurt another person. Yet I somehow managed to find my way through this 'dark night of the soul' – alone. Eventually, I discovered the work of Carl Jung and I began to realise that I was not possessed by evil; rather I was possessed by the unconscious and decades of split-off trauma and rage. I learnt a very deep lesson about meeting the shadow and how it is an integral part of the individuation process. Occasionally, I still encounter experiences of vulnerability and dissociation, but years of therapy and inner work have taught me how to process these 'complexes' and focus my energies on healing and wholeness.

My life-long journey as a wounded transformer inspired my vocation as a health professional and academic. I worked for twelve years as an occupational therapist in adult acute mental health services and also in a psychological therapies team, where I integrated a transpersonal approach into my clinical practice. I went on to work as a university lecturer for 10 years and my research focused on themes, such as spiritual crisis, transformative potential and spiritual renewal.

Throughout my life I have encountered various extremes, but I have also learnt that these challenges are thresholds for deep transformation. I never imagined as a 'confused child' that I would go on to gain a PhD and become a published author. My books: *The Unselfish Spirit* and *The Visionary Spirit* emerged phoenix-like from the ashes of my spiritual crisis. Becoming a writer has helped me articulate the complexities of individuation and the blessings of transformation. These days my quest for wholeness includes forgiving others and myself for past mistakes, as well as trying to be more grateful, charitable, just and loving. It's a soulful process and a work-in-progress.

*Lifton, B.J. (1994). Journey of the adopted self: A quest for wholeness. New York: Basic Books. Newton Verrier, N. (1993). The primal wound: Understanding the adopted child. Baltimore: Gateway Press.

# Jeannet is Kinda Proud of what her journey through NOTEs has taught her

*Jeannet, a Social Worker from Cambridge in the UK, has had a multitude of NOTEs. In this brave account, Jeannet explains how these, often inexplicable by logic, experiences have changed her forever. Like so many Experiencers recount, they have taken away her 'existential angst' and the common fear of death. We are so grateful to Jeannet for #EmergingProud to tell us about her extensive 'non-ordinary' journey....*

It is the night of 30 December, 1998. I am lying on the floor of a side-room in the star-shaped church of a Santo Daime community in the Amazon rainforest. I am lost in terror, beyond words, whimpering. This is the first of two NOTEs, 20 years apart, which involved a sense of possession by what felt like a dark 'entity', wanting to take me over.

These are extracts from what I wrote after the experience, which occurred during a plant medicine ceremony:-

"I started shaking badly, so I went to lie down. I got terrified. It felt like an entity was trying to take over my body. It came in different ways, contorting my face and body. I mostly remember it like octopus-like tentacles, engulfing me. After some time, it got to my heart. It felt like it was trying to take my soul away. Inwardly, I seemed to be told I should accept it, take it into myself. I was scared to but said 'I accept, for the love of God', and for a while kept repeating 'I accept'. At some point, I felt I needed to see what it was/look behind it. I really tried, and to hold love in my heart and remember everything is Light and terrors are fear of the Light, but I couldn't do it. This thing felt different. For a while I felt like it was strangling me, and I had a sharp pain in my heart. I started choking. There was a period when I felt myself sinking, going from rapid shallow breathing (like a bird that's dying) to not breathing at all; every so often remembering to breathe again with a gasp. I wanted to go to the Light, and caught glimpses of it, but I couldn't let myself go as I felt this thing was trying to get back in and so I couldn't leave myself unguarded."

Gradually the experience dissipated. As it was happening, I wondered if this was a split off part of myself: some part of my Shadow (as Carl Jung talks of it) that I should try to integrate, or if it was something bad with an independent existence that I should fight. I didn't know. This thing felt external and evil, or at least very toxic/dangerous – like it would kill me to get my body.

Afterwards, people told me I was facing my worst fears, as often happens with plant medicine. They reminded me that it's part of a process; a death/rebirth struggle. That I would get to a better place.

But how did I get here in the first place? I'd had an uneventful childhood. I did have a serious operation as a three-year-old which I can't remember, but which I think has left me with a fear of fully being present in my body. I was a shy and awkward only child, often retreating into books. I remember the inner crisis I felt when reading a book about Taoism in our loft, which in one swoop destroyed the image of the Christian God I had been taught. Later, in my teens, I wondered if I should just kill myself – if there wasn't more than material reality, I didn't want to live!

I had some experiences early on which may have been small NOTEs. There was, for instance, a powerful dream which may have warned me of my father's death (I didn't know he was ill), and later I heard a voice inside my head that wasn't mine asking me if I could cope if he died. The first time the answer that welled up in me was 'no'. The second time, 6 months later, it was 'yes'. My father died within the year. I shelved those experiences, as they didn't 'fit' with the materialist view of reality I grew up with.

There followed many years of longing to know there was 'more'. There were periods of searching (reading, meditation, attending groups, etc.), and periods of feeling numb to it all. Once, during a meditation, I saw the lower half of my body as a dragon, which scared me and stopped me meditating for a long time. I went through a range of life experiences: work, marriage and divorce, a complex, inappropriate relationship, bulimia, years of therapy, training as a counsellor and eventually training to be a social worker.

Then, in the summer of '97, I tried breathwork as a therapeutic tool, and had my first experience of full-blown NOTEs, including inner visions, a powerful heart opening and Kundalini energy flowing through my body. I trained as a breathwork facilitator and experimented with more natural hallucinogens. Both of these, together with changes in perception at times when Kundalini was active, have completely changed my view of who we are as human beings. I now know we are infinitely more than most of us in Western cultures think we are!

Those words in '98 - that I would get to a better place - came true. Some months later, in a transcendent journey, I had a NOTE that is hard to put into words. I experienced myself as a disembodied consciousness in a field of Consciousness, Love, Wisdom and infinite Compassion. I was part of it yet distinct, like a refraction in a crystal. I saw that there is nothing that is not that Light. I also found, to my surprise, that we are all completely known and deeply loved.

This experience has changed me forever. It's taken away my 'existential angst' and the fear I had of death. The message I was given was that we are all this Light and we should reflect it back to one another, so we can come to know it in ourselves. This is now the touch-stone in my life.

That was the end of this phase of inner work, although over the following 20 years there were periods when Kundalini energy was spontaneously activated in me, perhaps triggered by challenging life events. These episodes, usually lasting 1-2 months, also gave rise to NOTEs - some terrifying and some blissful, mostly during the night. In the last 2-3 years I have felt called to seek out further settings in which to experience NOTEs. I would always hit on inner terror but couldn't quite see what it was.

Then came my most recent breathwork session... Suddenly, there was the entity I had faced in Mapia. I felt terrified, but without thinking said "Okay, show yourself". I felt it enter my body and I had to fight my fear to not block it. Bit by bit it took me over until it reached my heart, causing sharp pain, and then my throat. I felt strangled and started wheezing badly. Finally, it took the whole of me. I was no longer thinking and just lived the experience as it took over my body. I felt my face contort into (what felt like) a daemonic expression, as my eyes rolled back and my voice sounded unrecognisable. I heard myself growling loudly. Gradually my terror turned to deep grief. Eventually the experience dissipated, and I came back to the room to listen to the music.

I don't fully understand what happened in that session, but I now trust more fully that (in a safe setting!) it is helpful to let a process run its course, even if you don't understand it and can't control what is happening. I have not felt anything 'bad' has lingered from it. I have felt more grounded and present in my body, and I have felt released from the sense, which had remained since that first experience, that there was something dangerous out there I couldn't see. Perhaps the question of whether something like that 'entity' is real or not cannot be answered – it was real for me. If it did have a degree of independent existence, it was also inextricably connected to me. We have both changed through this NOTE – maybe it's fair to say we have both been set free…

*Jeannet's conclusions from her experiences of things perhaps being unanswerable seems to be a great guide to what helps us get through these 'not-so-anomalous' experiences…Sitting with uncertainty, trying not to analyse them, and trusting and accepting the process. This is no easy task, but perhaps freedom comes when we learn to stop fighting and accept the darkness as an integral part of our human wholeness?*

# Julia from Slovakia #Emerges Proud to tell us about the transformative power of her NOTE

*Anyone who has experienced a NOTE knows just how transformative they can be; pulling us in a direction that once may have seemed illogical to the world we previously knew. Once you've been 'NOTE-ed' you just can't go back, and Julia Sellers from Slovakia knows all about that. Here Julia shares her personal account of her OBEs (out-of-body experiences): an essential component of NOTEs/STEs/EHEs*

I would like to share my story which began by having spontaneous out-of-body experiences (OBEs) many years ago. I consider OBEs a wonderful as well as an essential part of NOTEs/STEs/EHEs as long as you live the experience through your heart and Christ.

Anyway, it all started back in 1994 when I had my first OBE. At that time, I had no idea what was happening to me. All of my subsequent OBEs were therefore recorded in my diary so I could work with them later on. Basically, each of my OBEs was thoroughly written down immediately or shortly after it happened for further analysis.

This is how it all started back in 1994...

I remember waking up in the middle of the night. Without checking where I was located I knew I was in my bedroom but clearly out-of-body. I was hovering above my bed. Suddenly, something pulled me very strongly towards the window. I could not resist, even though I tried to with intention. I could not resist physically as I was out-of-body. I don't remember why I was pulled to the window as I could have been equally pulled through the wall or through the door. When out-of-body you easily pass through both walls as well as closed doors. I clearly heard my own breathing and my heart beating as if coming from a nearby radio.

Furthermore, I was able to hear everything that was going on in the next room as if I was present in the room. Suddenly, I was able to see a light coming from either the left or the right - I could not tell which, because when you are out of body, the sides sometimes get reversed like through a mirror - so the right is left and left is right. The light was getting more and more intense. I also remember I tried to raise my hand, however, I could not see any hand. My hand was a part of my real physical body laying on my bed at that time - what I saw was only the contours of my hand. It looked cloudy, shadowy, gaseous and I knew it was not a hand made of physical matter, flesh, muscles, and tissues. It was a phantom, an etheric double hand. At the point of looking at the phantom of my hand, I clearly thought to myself: "Get back to your body." And so I did, right after I intended to, with my mind.

Sound crazy? Well, shortly after my OBEs started, I kind of switched into a different mode of consciousness. You can call it altered, exceptional, anomalous, abnormal state of consciousness or, as I named it in one of my research papers: "State of Accreted Consciousness" (SAC). I was able to function in my "SAC" for over a year or so. I was not able to hold a job at that time, but guess what? I felt whole, integrated, transcended and deeply transformed during the whole period of my SAC. Furthermore, I clearly felt the presence of Christ and understood that people come to this wonderful planet to learn how to love.

I have come a long way since then. I have authored a book on OBEs (under the pseudonym of Iris Krst) titled: I Have Seen it Tomorrow. It is about the nature of OBEs, my own OBEs, but is mostly about the OBEs of a dear member of my family, who has experienced OBEs for over forty years now. He is not ready to come out of the spiritual closet yet. He needs some time to heal and understand that the gifts of OBE such as unitive consciousness, visionary experiences, ineffability, mystical and contemplative states, etc. which he was blessed with since birth, were deeply misunderstood by society and mistaken for a pathological condition by the medical community.

In addition, I have recently founded SEN Slovakia and the Czech Republic, which is part of ISEN (International Spiritual Emergence Network). I am also a lecturer on OBEs in the Czech Republic and Slovakia and counsel people with EHEs (Extraordinary Human Experiences) including NHI (Non-Human Intelligence ) contact modalities.

On my spiritual journey I have come to understand the following: You are what you feel, not what you think. Feelings come first. They produce thoughts. Feelings shape your whole being from within. Everything is feeling-based at its core. Feeling is sound/vibration-based. Vibration is feeling-based; oscillation is light-based. First, there was vibration in the form of audible or inaudible sound and only out of sound was light born. At the beginning, there was Logos: the word, the sound, the vibration. "In the beginning was the Word, and the Word was with God, and the Word was God." (The Bible, John 1:1)

By emitting feelings of unconditional love, you regulate your health and the ways your body functions. When you become unconditional love through Christ you become whole, integrated and fulfilled.

PLEASE JOIN ME IN BECOMING PURE UNCONDITIONAL LOVE.

Personal Bio:

I am a Lecturer, Author, Coach, Researcher, Counselor:

Born in Banovce nad Bebravou, in Western Slovakia (former Czechoslovakia), I experienced my first out-of-body experience in 1994. Since that time, I devote my free time to the study of autoscopic phenomena and other altered states of consciousness.

I have lectured in Slovakia, the Czech Republic, and the U.S.A. I have appeared in national, as well as international, media. I hold three degrees in: Russian Area Studies, Adult Pedagogy, and Law. I am a reviewer for PLOS ONE, the world's first multidisciplinary Open Access scientific peer-reviewed journal. I hold a certificate in Abnormal Psychology and I am pursuing a diploma in Divinity.

*Find out more about Julia here: www.juliasellers.sk*
*And SEN Slovensko a Česko (part of ISEN): http://www.*
*spiritualemergencenetwork.org/slovakia*

## A Near-Death Experience aged 4 led to a lifetime of study; to make the so called 'paranormal' normal

*Meet Sperry Andrews, founder/co-director of the Human Connection Institute. From an N.D.E. at age 4, his background is in physics, neuroscience, philosophy, (para)psychology, art and art history, healing, mysticism, and filmmaking. He has explored two-way telepathic awareness internationally with hundreds of groups for over thirty years.*

*Here Sperry gives you a glimpse of his younger experiences that led to his incredible work…*

When I was thirty-two, after a year living in Western Australia, I moved to Hobart, Tasmania.

I was then at the same latitude South as my birthplace was North. The presence of Antarctica taught me there can be radiant cold. Its icy presence pierced my bones, until it seemed like they could snap.

I took a plane North up the coast to Cairns, North Queensland and found a free ashram in Mount Molloy - up in the tablelands - run by an English couple. They gave me a garden shed to live in on the edge of their property where I could meditate without being disturbed.

I felt an overpowering need to do absolutely nothing other than be awake and aware. When taking walks out into the bush, I'd sit for long stretches. The more still I became inside, the more Nature came alive.

A couple of months passed and I settled down. One night I was reading a passage from Jiddu Krishnamurti wherein he suggested to make "no effort." I felt compelled to experience effortlessness. By the next morning, having laid awake all night, without need of sleep, a turgid cloud of psychic matter gathered in front of my face - a few inches away. It seemed to contain all that I had withdrawn my attention from, all of what I had not been conscious of until then.

It was awesome to be hallucinating my 'disowned' self. I'd never experienced anything like it before. There was a mental/emotional, as well as physical desire, to

74

turn away from 'it'.

By sustaining effortless awareness, within the space of a minute or two, the cloud dissolved into the awareness I was witnessing it with. Free from what I had hidden from, who and what I knew myself to be became infused with the radical presence of impersonal awakeness. This continued throughout the day and into the night. And then suddenly, as if by magic, I lost all limitations, becoming a boundaryless Void; seemingly the source of all possibilities and potentialities, without beginning or end.

Everything was made of this one consciousness. Sounds outside my body also seemed to come from inside of me. There was not one place within that did not contain everything and nothing. The most serene bliss came over every cell in my body and heart. My mind was utterly silent. I was indistinguishable from all I was perceiving.

I was not any one thing, yet I was this universe, unfolding as a spaceless timeless awakeness. Stepping outside into the night, I decided it was as good a time as any to go look at a used car I'd seen in the paper. The owners lived over an hour away and I had no phone to call them. I decided to do something I'd not done since I arrived. I walked to the one and only road, to hitch a ride to a phone.

At eight or nine at night, standing on the side of an empty road, there were no cars. The moon and stars were high overhead, yet they felt every bit as much inside me too. Throughout all this, there were no thoughts, only direct perceptions.

I felt and saw the moon was as much in my knee as it was in my heart and hands. There was a distinct sense that the whole universe was within every part of my being - this vast formless, featureless awakeness. It was then I saw a car's headlights in the distance and I had one of my first and only thoughts.

I wondered, innocently, "Wouldn't it be nice if this person stopped their car, picked me up and took me to Atherton," an hour away. The car approached and its brakes engaged, bringing it - skidding on the dirt - to a sudden halt next to me. A small Japanese woman rolled down her window, seemingly disoriented. "Where are you going?" she asked.

When I told her, she added that she lived just up the road, but she'd take me (two hours out of her way). It was uncanny, though it felt right somehow. Once in the car, I could feel her sensing the effect of our presence. As she started to drive, she asked: "What are you doing?"

I answered, saying: "I'm just noticing, I am everything I'm conscious of." Energetically, I could feel her recognize our combined consciousness. All she said was, "oh." Then there was only one of us. We both clearly sensed the sound of each others' words actually arising from within our common body.

She told me how frightened she had been of everyone, as her husband had brought her here from Japan to live, and she knew no one. That her neighbor from time to time would take care of her newborn baby. She explained how she suffered terribly from thoughts of her neighbor intending harm to her child. Asking, did I think it was true or not, I said I did not sense it was, and we entered into a deeper peace together.

We maintained a unified consciousness all the way to Atherton. Before dropping me off, we stopped and shared something to eat while we waited for the car owner to come get me. She and I agreed to meet again in a few days' time, and said good night.

The couple selling the car invited me to spend the night. It was a forty mile round-trip for them to come and get me. Back at their home, they sat me down and started sharing their deepest conflicts. She said he kicked their cows. Then asked, what did I suggest they do about it.

Both of them were on the edge of their seats hanging on my every word and movement. I had certainly never experienced anything like this, yet it flowed so effortlessly. I was acceptance itself. Reflecting their dilemma seemed to bring clarity and they felt remarkably resolved.

It was after 11 when they showed me to a room with a bed. When I closed my eyes, I did not sleep. It was like being the night sky - light years in every direction - but instead there was only the sparkling beauty of pure objectless consciousness. The night passed without dreams, as if time did not exist.

When I opened my eyes again, the manifest universe re-appeared around me. This quality of experience lasted for several days. I found I could move in and out of 'it' by noticing I was everything and everyone I was witnessing – or not.

A week later, I was no longer in this consciousness. I was back to being just a separate self again. The Japanese woman came over to take me out to lunch. She was so tense, she felt like she was electrified with fear.

To make a long story shorter, we were not able to communicate in the way we had, and eventually she became so scared she could not stand to be around me. I had to hitch a ride 'home'. The insecurity of being 'unconscious together' seemed almost unbearable for her. It saddened me.

The difference between that one night and this day a week later was astounding. I was so profoundly moved by how she had picked up a total stranger - a 6'2" man nonetheless, on a lonely road at night - to drive him two hours out of her way. The only difference was the quality of 'my' consciousness. If I'd been more awake, she'd have been able to relax. I unmistakably realized from this experience I was wholly responsible for ending fear in relationship. That how awake I am is more important than anything else I might do or say.

Personal Bio:

From an NDE (near-death experience) at four, and as an experiential scientist since 1983, I have been demonstrating humanity's capacity to share a commonly-sensed consciousness. As an adjunct research associate of the Mind Science Foundation, I collaborated with Dr. William Braud to pioneer laboratory research which helped to establish the field of Distant Mental Influence on Living Systems (DMILS). Publishing in peer-reviewed journals and presenting on human interconnectedness at public and professional organizations - including the United Nations - I orchestrated a multinational, scientifically based, media project to produce and direct documentaries and feature films to further the evolution of a socially altruistic, heart-centered intelligence. To gain access to these deeper levels of compassionate insight and two-way telepathic awareness, I have been facilitating hundreds of groups internationally for over thirty years. I have learned to teach anyone interested how to effectively recreate these experiences in-person, or online via webcam.

*Find out more at: www.connectioninstitute.org*
*Join free online gatherings at*
*www.consciousness-quotient.com/knowing-sharing-awareness-consciously-together/*

# Sabine from the Netherlands is Kinda Proud of how her shamanic calling has been her mental saviour

*Sabine Obermayr-Adamzek, from Switzerland, currently living in the region Arnhem, The Netherlands, graciously tells us how her shamanic calling to be a healer manifested through what the western world calls 'psychosis'. We see more and more proof that it is high time we 're-think mental illness' through these stories. Thank you Sabine, for sharing your journey...*

## Shamanism, my key to mental sanity

Writing this story was inspired by the documentary Crazywise, by Phil Borges and Kevin Tomlinson. I dare to state that shamanism saved my mental sanity. By now I am living with a worldview that is strongly based on knowledge and tools from indigenous people.

### Burkina Faso

A few months after my 28th birthday I found myself breathing deeply, for the first time in my life, the nocturnal air of Africa. I was standing on a platform on top of the stairs that lead down onto the tarmac of the airport of Ouagadougou, the capital of Burkina Faso, a small country in West Africa.

Little did I know that this visit would change my life fundamentally and irreversibly.

I was invited, as one of the members of an international group of people, by Sotigui Kouyaté (19 July 1936 – 17 April 2010), the head of a clan of griots and griottes that are part of the Mandinka ethnic group. Griots and griottes are keepers of the oral tradition: storytellers, singers, performers, dancers and actors.

A number of westerners from a variety of countries, including me, were scheduled to travel around with several members of the Kouyaté family to do research for a theater project. I was a professional actress at that time.

To make a long story short: during this trip I started to have, what a professional would call, psychotic episodes. I saw things that others didn't see, I heard strange voices in my head and I generally felt out of sorts, especially in the countryside. I remember a very strong physical sensation of dissolving into the earth, not being able to breathe anymore: it felt like being underwater, drowning in the earth. It seemed that I had senses that weren't there before I went to Africa. I was feeling things happening miles away, hearing rock formations talking to me in my head...

I can assure you it felt absolutely terrifying. I lost my sense of self, my identity of who I was. On the other hand, I had experiences of being part of something much larger than mankind, that infused my mind and my body with a sense of wellbeing that I hadn't encountered before and left me totally confused. I convinced myself, there and then, that these feelings and sensations were related to my extended stay in Africa, and that they would vanish as soon as I was back in Switzerland, where I lived and worked at that time.

Guess what...They didn't!

### Back in Zürich

After having returned to Zürich (Switzerland) a number of weeks later, these feelings, sensations and voices in my head still kept me awake various nights and made my daily life, and functioning the way I used to function, very difficult.

I remember one morning where I found myself sitting at the base of a big tree in a forest nearby the town center, soaked with rainwater to my skin and disoriented; gazing confused into the friendly face of a forest worker who asked me if I was alright. I answered more automatically than consciously: "Yes, of course", but obviously I wasn't.

I had absolutely no recollection of how I ended up there. I had a vague memory of incredibly complicated energetic structures and deep friendly voices in my head. If anyone would have asked me then what I remembered, I would have stared at them blankly and would have answered: "Nothing".

At that point in time I was terrified; shaken to my core by the feeling of absolute powerlessness. Being in the grip of something so much bigger than me that had taken over my consciousness. I wept for the woman that I had been, and wasn't looking forward to the person I was becoming.

Losing my memory, my sense of self and not knowing where all these weird experiences would bring me, I decided that it was time to seek out a psychiatrist. A few weeks later my psychiatrist told me that I should take medication to control my ongoing psychotic episodes. I was afraid of what these chemicals would do to me and my brain and decided to look for an alternative solution.

In the years that followed that episode, the knowledge that was dropped in my head that night started to surface at appropriate times and gave me a lot of insight about the mechanics of the universe and the interconnection of all living systems. Synchronistically, I came into contact with a Dutch man who was practicing Shamanism in France. After our initial contact on the phone, he told me that he was expecting me: that his Spirits had already informed him that a Swiss lady would seek his help, and he recognized me as this person. He invited me to participate in his upcoming workshop, where we would find the time to consult the spirit world concerning my problems.

### Shamanism and shamanic illness

In the first workshop I attended he taught me several techniques to regain control over what was happening to my mind. He promised me ongoing teaching and mentoring to follow my calling. "What calling?" I asked him.

He explained to me that, from a shamanic point of view, certain types of "mental illness" may be nothing more than a strong calling to develop and research certain abilities that would be beneficial, not only for the person who is experiencing this "illness", but for everybody and everything this person would encounter later in life. That this experience - this "illness" - is an inherent part of the training to become a shaman, a mediator between worlds. This training would not only involve himself as a teacher but, more importantly, there would be other teachers from unseen realms that would guide me in my search.

He would teach me how to reach out to these teachers, to learn how to integrate the messages from the other worlds and train me to balance what was going on in my life in a good, healthy way. That I would embark on a journey with him to become a shamanic practitioner. For 15 years I worked with Daan van Kampenhout as his student and co-teacher.

I was reading, studying and practicing all kinds of indigenous and tribal worldviews from Lakota to Sami: from real people, healers and medicine people, to knowledge that continues to be passed on to me in dreams and trance journeys, since 1995.

### Interconnectedness

Praying, like traditional medicine people do, accepting my "gift" of being able to communicate with everything that lives, and generally embracing the idea that we are all interconnected with everything that has a spirit, the visible and unseen world around us, all coming from a common source - the creator - confirmed a lot of what I experienced in my 'psychotic' episodes.

Humility, deep felt gratitude and compassion are, since then, a constant factor in my life. They form the basis of my work as a shamanic practitioner and systemic facilitator.

*In #Emerging Proud, we like to call this the 'positive domino effect' - with every person who is brave enough to step up, accept their calling and work on personal healing, becoming able to offer support to others on the same path. It's thanks to Sabine's bravery, intense study and self-work that she is now able to do just that...*

*Sabine's website: www.desystemischeblik.nl*

# When Rohini had been squeezed under too much life pressure it allowed her Star Self to be born

*When Rohini, from Pennsylvania, USA, experienced 'unusual symptoms', she asked a stranger on a helpline: "Am I going mad?" This astute reply: "No sweetie, you are not going mad, you are having an awakening", changed her life forever. Ro now wants to spread awareness of spiritual awakening in order to help others who may also have gone through a process of falling apart - to know that this may actually be the start of you becoming who you truly are and living a joyful life. What a star she is!*

*This is Rohini's inspiring story through trauma to emergence...*

## A Star is Born

Scientists say, when atoms of light elements are squeezed under enough pressure for their nuclei to undergo fusion, a star is born. I am sure my parents didn't think of this when they named me Rohini. They probably named me after the Hindu astrology star, Rohini.

In the majority of cases, when a girl is born in India, she is considered a liability and treated like one: I was no different. Things were hard for me, with my brother being exceptionally brilliant and me being just average. He became my parents' favorite child, and I a source of humiliation. In my twenties, I was in a relationship with a guy whose parents despised me because I belonged to the lowest of castes as per the Indian caste system, called the "untouchables". Against much resistance we got married and moved to America. While all this was happening, my brother was slipping away. After graduating from an Ivy league college, he quit his high-paying, prestigious job, abandoned his family and left for the Himalayas. On his return, he abused drugs, tried to commit suicide, had no control over his behavior and disowned us.

He was soon diagnosed with schizophrenia. This broke our family, each one of us in a different way. The whole family spiraled into acute depression. A cloud of suicidal thoughts, denial, anger, sadness, agony, depression and numbness loomed over us for years. While this was playing out, my entry into the new family turned abusive in the first week of marriage. Following years of repression, I filed for divorce. My world had grown very dark and lonely.

About 6 months after my divorce, I met a guy – it was the start of a very turbulent few months, as he was separated but still married. My association with him was against everything I ever believed to be true about myself. I then unexpectedly became pregnant and he walked out on us.

I was in a foreign country, abandoned by my ex-husband for whom I had left my home behind, abandoned by my family who told me never to come back to India, and abandoned by my lover. I knew that I did not want my baby to feel this abandonment. I went ahead and got an abortion.

I had failed as a daughter, I had failed as a sister, I had failed as a wife, I had failed as a lover, and I had chosen to fail in the unexpected role of a mother. I had failed at being a WOMAN. I spiraled into acute suicidal depression, the trauma was too much to bear. I was getting ready to kill myself.

Something changed soon after I made the decision: the heaviness, the hate, the darkness, the burden lifted. I felt light. I continued to make plans to kill myself, but I felt different in my heart. My mind was telling me to act differently. I was scared.

While talking to a friend, sensing my erratic behavior they yelled at me, "Oh stop! Just stop with all this spiritual bullshit!" I was stunned - the word "spiritual" triggered something in me, this word didn't exist in my personal dictionary. What did this word, "spiritual" mean? So, I opened my laptop and typed the word "Spiritual". The phrase "Spiritual Awakening" appeared in my search box and I hit enter.

I read through some blogs and watched a few videos. I felt crazy. These were the very symptoms I had been experiencing the last few months. As I looked at my reflection in the mirror my whole world collapsed...I was itching all over my body: my head, my neck, my arms. I looked around my bathroom: everything merged into each other, everything blended into one, everything was just particles and particles of light... just a shimmering soft color of yellow. Everything was ONE. I was unable to distinguish between the mirror, the lights, the shower curtain or the walls... everything was just a blend of light. It was like I was seeing different colors blend into one color on a paint palette. Everything was one light.

As I continued to look at the mirror, deep into my own eyes, I remembered that I was wearing this body like a piece of cloth for a role I had come here to play, as a woman. I remembered that I was not this mere body: I was not the mind, which kept yelling at me to kill myself, but I was that feeling, that knowing, that unconditional fountain of love that flooded my heart and my whole being in this very moment. I felt the joy of my being. I remembered that I was just a speck of dust but, at the same time, I was the entire universe in motion. And I laughed - I laughed for a long time and, with that laughter, I was liberated from my suffering.

After a while I got scared. I was experiencing an indescribable feeling of being flooded with love, compassion, empathy and joy for myself. But, my body continued to itch and I was seeing spots of light. I was not able to comprehend what was happening: I thought maybe I was going crazy. I was 33 and suicidal. Maybe this was the onset of schizophrenia, like my brother? As I grew frantic, I googled for "help during a Spiritual Awakening" and I came across ACISTE (American Center for the Integration of Spiritually Transformative Experiences) and called their helpline number…it went to a voicemail.

My skin was peeling off of my body and I felt like I would burst into a million pieces from this indescribable feeling in my heart. As I was panicking, a lady called me back from ACISTE. She asked me what was going on. I started a verbal frenzy. The lady patiently listened and, after I was done, I asked her, "What is happening to me? Am I going mad? Should I call 911?" She said, "No sweetie, you are not going mad, you are having an awakening". Those words changed my life forever.

December 5th, 2016. This day was my real birthday: the day of my rebirth, with the feeling and knowing of my true nature. The day I woke up from the dream. The day I shed thousands and thousands of years of old skin and realized my pure essence. And, for the first time in my life, I appreciated the beauty of my body,

I felt unconditional love overflowing from my heart and I felt the serenity of my being. I was free from the suffering of my mind. I was just joyous for being - and for being me. For the first time in my life, I was happy to be ALIVE. I was in that euphoric state for months and, with the help of a couple of amazing people, I slowly integrated the transformation into my life.

Divine grace touched my heart and my heart flooded with unconditional love. There was only NOW and there was only God, as all of us. I realized I was God and everyone else was God as well. To this realization, I am eternally grateful.

I now know that everything and everyone is one energy; we are only separated by what we think.

And, that is how this star was born.

**Amanda is Kinda Proud that she learnt to connect to the true authentic expression of herself, and BE it unapologetically.**

*More often than not it can take an existential crisis to discover who we truly are, beneath all of our old coping mechanisms that we use to repress pain we are not ready to feel. Amanda shares how her life crisis has turned out to be her biggest blessing; it has led her to discover who she truly is, and not only is she living her authentic version of herself, she has finally learned to love herself too!*

Rise up in Love; Connect to the magic of Hummingbird and the sweet nectar of life.

My journey of falling in love with myself began when my 17-year relationship and marriage broke down and, ultimately, came to an end. My entire life as I knew it had fallen apart.

Shortly after the separation, I discovered certain truths that led me to feel deceived and betrayed. The rejection I felt was gut-wrenching. The whole situation brought up my old story of feeling unlovable and replaceable:

My heart shattered into a million pieces.

It felt like my life had ended.

It felt like someone had died.

It felt like I had lost a part of my body.

I was totally heartbroken.

I felt unworthy.

I felt ashamed.

I felt like a failure.

I felt scared.

I felt guilty.

The list of self-loathing emotions I felt towards myself was endless.

For a long while, getting out of bed in the morning was the biggest struggle.

I felt hopeless, a terrible mother, my body was gripped in such deep grief and pain that I literally felt like I couldn't move. I couldn't even think about tomorrow without feeling anxious and panicky.

Over the years I had developed an addiction to recreational drugs which I felt so much shame over. I didn't really know how to go out and enjoy myself without it.

I had no idea who I was.

I hadn't supported myself financially for 14 years. At 42 years old, I had no idea how to start a new life on my own. But deep down inside I had a knowing…A knowing that this was right and happening for me. A knowing that this was an opportunity to rise up and connect to my authentic self.

I remember the day that woke me up and urged me to begin rebuilding myself and my life.

I was in bed and had barely been out of my room for a while. My daughter came over and made me get up and go see a friend. When I got back later, she had gone, my house was spotless and on my freshly made bed was a note saying: 'Tomorrow is a new day. I love you.' I sobbed as my heart filled with love and gratitude for the love, beauty, compassion and wisdom she had shown me. My baby girl, now a young woman, had reminded me of love - unconditional love - and I decided at that moment to begin my journey back to loving myself.

I had to for my children.

I had to for myself.

It has been 2 years from the life I knew falling apart, to sitting here sharing my story.

In these 2 years, I have become a Forrest Yoga teacher, a bodyworker and healer, a transformational life coach. I moved and created a beautiful new home for myself and my kids. I started my own business, I met my twin flame, and most importantly I have fallen deeply in love with myself and my life. When I look back, I feel so much gratitude, so much pride, at how far I've come.

So how did I do it? How did I turn my life around?

First, I made a commitment that no matter what, I was going to stay in a place of love and live from my heart.

I learnt to stop living in the past, repeating stories, and instead create a beautiful new life.

I learnt to receive and give love unconditionally.

I learnt to forgive myself and everyone else involved.

I learnt to connect to the true authentic expression of me and BE it unapologetically.

I committed to leading by example and show my children that it is possible to rise above anger, resentment and bitterness into unconditional love.

I committed to living with integrity and grace.

I committed to loving harder than any other negative emotion, embody and BE love.

Second, I chose to take responsibility for what had happened in my life, for my own happiness, and not play into victimhood and drama anymore.

To be responsible for and change my behaviour, habits and stories connected to the imprints of my past that were clearly no longer serving me.

I overcame my addictions to drama, behaviour and stories of a lifetime. I had to get clear and conscious of what they were in order to catch myself, interrupt the pattern and change it.

Third, I practiced dreaming about how I wanted my future to look.

How I wanted to feel.

Who I wanted to be.

What I wanted to do.

Why I wanted to do it.

I practiced and embodied how my future self would act, feel and be and made a commitment to BE that person every day. I learnt tools to support me to overcome those moments when my past self would try and draw me back.

Every day I practiced, committed and invested wholeheartedly into being my future self until it was more of a habit than being my past self. And when I fell from grace, I owned it, made amends, forgave myself, loved myself and started again. I chose to never give up.

I surrendered to the deeply uncomfortable and painful emotions I had repressed my whole life; I leaned right into vulnerability.

I chose to rise up out of victimhood and into empowerment.

I chose to embody and FEEL deep gratitude and love for every experience, not only the joyful ones.

I chose to open my heart fully and commit to living, breathing and being my future self every single day.

*Amanda is based in Norwich, UK, where she lives and works. Her work is about empowering her clients in their own healing, in order to fall in love with oneself and their life - rising up in love and living from the heart. Amanda holds classes, workshops, courses, retreats, in person and online. She also works one-on-one with clients, empowering them in their healing and in their lives.*

*Amanda's Website: http://thehummingbirdproject.co*

# Take NOTE from Dave - the challenges of awakening

*Dave's story is resonant of the patterns inherent in most spiritual awakening experiences: deep existential questioning in childhood, followed by an ineffable experience of 'Oneness' with the love of the Universe which completely transforms our world view. This blissful experience often leads to despair, due to a struggle to explain the experience to others, and the pressure to continue to conform to a society that feels too restrictive as a result. These experiences can be isolating if we can't find others who understand and to whom we can relate, hence the importance of communities such as #EmergingProud and the bravery*

This story began long before I had any memories, but the primary and most powerful experience was forty-five years ago. I was eighteen and had become absorbed in the deep distress of my friend, at one point spending a continuous seven hours wondering how she had become so distressed and what could possibly be of any assistance. I knew I could not help in any real way - I had poor confidence and communication skills, little experience of life, and did not know who to turn to. But I strongly felt that help was needed and had to be provided somehow.

Through a long car journey and then sitting alone in my room, this question must have turned into a deep and wordless prayer, reaching a point where I was lifted entirely out of myself into the underlying reality of existence. This was so "other-worldly" that it did not register on my conscious mind; my everyday self was sitting on a chair but I was immersed in a primary aspect of the cosmos. For a timeless period I was gone.

Slowly, I started to return to my body and I began to feel some after-effects of the realm where I had been taken: an extraordinary bliss and power, a fathomless depth of love manifesting in the material and immaterial realms. Effortlessly energising all substance, consciousness and movement, the radiation of an incredible love powers every aspect of existence.

Not having any words to describe this, I just stayed with it. My entire outlook on life completely changed.

Sometimes I saw a person's interpenetrating psychic layers, full of complexity and meaning in slow, or quicker, movement. Each of us so absorbed in our own concerns that we couldn't see the extraordinary wonder of life. Adults were especially unaware of the energetic layers of their psyche, disconnected from so much of their being. Yet if those energies had not been there, the physical body would have just collapsed; slowly disintegrating into a formless puddle.

There I was, without any direction about what to do with it all. With an underlying blissfulness I just followed routines, believing if I kept quiet it would create less disturbance. Meanwhile, I tried to find out what was going on: thinking, 'how is it everyone is so imprisoned in themselves?' Feeling high and relaxed, I went to school and wondered why it was important that I should isolate myself in my brain and work with ideas that had no direct relevance to the underlying realities in life. Coming home again I kept an inner distance from my family, unable to share my experience in a way that communicated something of its nature. Any time I started to open up about this experience the response was dense and confused, missing the quality of the experience entirely. I couldn't find the right words at all.

About three months later I was more or less in an everyday state of mind again. My friend was doing better and I wondered about whether to share all this with her. Rightly or wrongly, I also felt she would not appreciate the wonder of it and would think I had lost my mind somehow. So I went on searching for someone who knew. I read many books and went to churches; I was disappointed to see many religious people talking about holy things without really connecting to them, without living it in a moment by moment experience. The search became more desperate as my ignorantly practiced bad habits began to bring me down.

Eventually I opened a tatty little book that had been lying around for some time: *Knowledge of the Higher Worlds and its Attainment,* by Rudolf Steiner. I drank in this book that had originally looked so unappealing - it spoke to me! I became aware that the person who wrote that book knew exactly what he was talking about. I felt wonderfully reassured and refreshed. I did not understand the book, yet it felt utterly authentic. Steiner had provided an instruction manual for inner development, one that took account of the different dimensions of human existence in the modern age. So I relaxed, thinking I would get round to doing the exercises he recommended sometime in the future, and re-engaged with ordinary teenage existence.

Lacking confidence in the everyday world, and without any sense of what occupational role I should get involved with, I lived day-to-day simply believing that applying myself to spiritual practice and maintaining my independence was enough. Aimless and easily led, I also discounted much of everyday life, thinking the spiritual was more essential. Over-doing meditative practices, in particular, led me to be ungrounded and unaware of the ordinary realities, including how my ordinary personality worked. This meant I had a poor memory, was intermittently sensitive, and was rarely "fully present" in ordinary life.

Independent and rather isolated, I floated through jobs and different situations, negotiated changes, travelled, studied and gained a wide range of experience. In my thirties I felt I needed to become more involved with life. Eventually, I found an occupational role that suited me – I got married, had children and a health service career.

As I finally practice some of Steiner's exercises, I begin to see how much I have missed in life. Yet maybe that needed to happen before I could freely and consciously apply myself to self-improvement. Although I am now deliberately strengthening it, my will-power is still not good enough to balance my thinking and feeling, and I remain vulnerable to drifting into murky waters.

I have become wary of the direction of my thoughts and passions; I know these can mislead me. Patiently, I need to acquire the ability to take charge of my inner life: to learn how to strengthen it against self-importance, materialism and other psychological, spiritual and cultural influences. I need to fully appreciate the people around me and the contribution they make to our development. Nowadays, the possibility exists of not being continuously swept up in the dramas of everyday life, but being open to a subtle inner guidance informing my selection of what to see, what to do, and how to go about it.

Although I remain in my spiritual infancy, and fall over all the time, there is some progress. When I fully pay attention to each clink of the washing up I hear an extraordinary symphony of incidental music. The calls of the seagulls echo with infinite desolation, or contentment, or irritation, in their fight over food. People are by far the most amazing; how is it that what we say we say, and what we do we do, out of all the things that could be said and done? And through the whole wide world, every psychic movement in each individual is lovingly overseen, in a transcendent framework of developmental opportunity.

*As Dave clearly demonstrates, the spiritual evolution journey is continuous post 'wake-up', and integrating the spiritual and human aspects of ourselves is so vital...being mindful and grateful for each moment of life as much as we can be can certainly help with the process.*

# French Canadian Diane's Kundalini awakening led her to shed her identity with her 'mental illness' label

*Diane's experience is unfortunately all too common in Western society today; she received a diagnosis of being 'mentally ill' without the context for her emotions being explored at all. When we are able to consider her experience of emotional instability in terms of the life pressures that preceeded it, it seems much more understandable and actually a natural consequence. Thankfully Diane was able to find her own way out, ironically by going 'within'...*

### "Know Thyself" – Socrates

**"It is no measure of health to be well adjusted
to a profoundly sick society."
Jiddu Krishnamurti**

My name is Diane Gagné, I'm 49 years old and mother
of 2 beautiful young adults of 21 and 19 years old.
I've been married 25 years to a wonderful man, my
"guardian angel," as I like to call him.

When I was a child, I was very imaginative - always
in my comic books, a very enthusiastic kid. I grew
up in a family where I was alone with my parents
because my brother, who was 18 years older than
me, had already left the family home. My father was
older than my friends' fathers and I was a privileged
person. I was very happy all the time and a little bit
blind to the jealousy of my friends. So, when at 9, I
began menstruating and started to grow up to become
a woman over approximately 6 months, I didn't notice
the attention of the boys on me and the jealousy of my
friends. I started to be bullied; the end of my time at
primary school, and the beginning of my time at high
school, were very tough. When I was 16, my father
died of cancer. It was very painful and I "crashed" for
the first time.

I met my husband at age 18, but we had to live
separately during our studies. When we finally settled
down together it was very very far from our hometown,
because my husband was posted there, and after that
received an offer to start a business with partners. So

we decided to make our life an 8 hour drive away from our families. We raised our child alone with no help most of the time, and with 2 careers this was difficult to balance. I was a lawyer and I worked most of my career as a Crown Attorney. I struggled a lot to balance job and family, and a very sensitive part of me - a part that was having a lot of trouble dealing with the misery that I was seeing in my job, as I dealt with a lot of cases related to sexual assault and physical abuse on children.

At 35 years old I received a bipolar disorder diagnosis and I started to take medication. Lots of different medication was tried. I had a hard time with medication and with trying to stabilize my moods. I was always flitting between depression and hypomanic states. I never had psychosis but a lot of little manic states where I was very high, irritable and spent a lot of money. In 2010 I changed my job and worked in human resources. This was a less stressful, 4 days a week, job. It was better, but not so much. In 2013 I started to practice running and it helped too, but I had an intestinal obstruction in 2014 and almost died from it. I had to stop running for a few months and 1 year later I had to stop again for a hernia. Each time I stopped running, I experienced a little depression. All this "mess" built up in 2016 when I had a mixed state: depression and manic symptoms at the same time. It was horrible and, in July of that year, I made a suicide attempt.

Someone didn't seem to want me yonder but, after that, I was completely lost. Lost, weak and I didn't know what to do with my life. I had memory breaks, difficulty concentrating and other cognitive difficulties, so I started to meditate. I was ready to try everything to help me. But I was a skeptical person, really down to earth, and I stopped believing in God after the death of my father. When I was young I was practicing - close to God and Jesus - but when I lost my father, I closed the door on religion.

Anyway, meditation was very difficult at the beginning, I was unable to concentrate on music or guided meditation. So, after a few days, I threw all this away and I decided to just listen. Listen inside, to all those thoughts spinning all the time in my head... I listened; I became conscious of them more and more every day and rapidly, one day, they stopped. They stopped for a few minutes and they started again! But, I realized that it was always the same thoughts playing like a tape in my head. And, during that little break to rewind the tape, something "magic" started to happen. I felt something inside me, a kind of energy flowing from the bottom of me, rising in my head, and the feeling was incredible! I felt calm, at peace. So, I started to meditate more and more. After a few months of that, I started to have some strange experiences of voices and guidance in my meditations and a few weeks after that I experienced a Kundalini awakening.

Since then, my life has completely changed, for the better...but also the worst at the beginning! It was, at first, a complete change of perspective on life in just a few days, a huge break on the ego and the emerging of a new state of consciousness. But also a lot of psychic manifestations, quite similar to a psychosis state. I flitted between those two states for many months and when I started to realize what was really happening to me: a spiritual awakening, I started to live it, in the most troubling way for me - in the mystic way. I experienced an enormous call to God, something that I really didn't understand and something very conflicting for me, as I didn't believe anymore in God. In almost 2 years, slowly but surely, I broke all my skepticism and my conditioning about my beliefs in life, but mainly my beliefs about myself. I discovered that I was not that sick person that I had become over the years, completely identified with my diagnosis. I was not that person who always did what people expected of me. And I was not that unconfident person, dragging her guilt and her sadness like a second skin.

I discovered, as days passed, that I am a light - a beautiful shining light, living her life free of all conditioning and wanting to help people to do the same thing - to help others discover what we all have inside of us.

We are all connected to life in a way that we cannot imagine, and some people feel that connection at a deeper level, an unconscious one, in a way that can manifest as suffering. With time, they can become disconnected from themselves, which causes more suffering or increased manifestations like voices or visions.

After 2 years travelling into conscience, I completely changed my perception of mental illness and want to say this to people suffering in life:

*You are not alone - in fact, you have the whole universe inside you!*

With help, a lot of work on yourself and patience, you can discover this beautiful gift inside you. If I did it, you can. Slowly but surely, one day at a time, you can discover your own light and make it shine in your life. Find your path and an exit from mental suffering. This experience was extremely difficult and confusing for me: I struggled with visions, voices and many manifestations; I rediscovered God. But finally, at the end, I found peace and joy and, especially, I found my true self.

*When we identify with any labels of 'mental illness' that are bestowed on us from external powers, that is where our journey ends. But as Diane's story demonstrates, as do so many more, if we are able to shed these labels and discover ourselves as an infinite essence of pure consciousness, then our potential is unrestricted and infinite.*

# Wendy is Kinda Proud of the wisdom of her body following a near death experience

*Wendy Andrews from Queensland, Australia emerges proud to tell us how it took somatic release therapy for her mind to catch up with the wisdom of her body, years after a traumatic experience. Wendy's experience is not uncommon, although not yet widely recognised. It's through sharing our stories, such as Wendy does here, that we can raise awareness and give hope to those who may still be stuck in suffering. As Wendy's discovery shows, it can be so validating to find out the reasons behind our emotional responses, as sometimes that is all it takes to set us back onto the upward spiral*

*of self- acceptance.*

I want to write about what was, for me, a very powerful healing session, and its follow up session, recently. I've been clearing away the detritus of my past for almost thirty years using, mainly, emotional release work in listening partnerships. The labels I've used to find information and research are 'complex PTSD', 'panic disorder', and 'agoraphobia'. I experienced childhood sexual assaults and started having what were treated as 'epileptic seizures' in my late teens, but which turned out to be a body response to trauma overload.

My intention was to increase the sense of capacity for stress in my nervous system, to grow the 'window of tolerance', as it's referred to, using Somatic Experiencing, with a trained Practitioner. I'd had two sessions with this Practitioner in person, and then switched to Skype. I started by noticing what was going well, for instance, I talked about the chaotic things that had happened in my home over the previous few days and how I wasn't reaching overwhelm as quickly as I would have in the past. It took a few days to reach that point, rather than a few minutes.

A memory had come to my mind a few times and I mentioned it because, as unrelated to anything as it seemed, over the years, I've learned to trust what 'pops up'. I'd gone in to have my wisdom teeth removed, somewhere around the age of 18. I had a general anaesthetic in a small surgery one Saturday morning. I'd only briefly met the dentist once before. The way I remember being told afterward, I'd had to be given extra paralysing grains by the anaesthetist, as it wasn't working properly, but eventually I went under (I do remember excruciating pain in my thumbs as I counted down).

The next thing I knew, I was being brought around. Apparently, my nails had turned blue and the operation had to be aborted, even though they had all the tubes down my throat and were about to take out the teeth. Because of the extra paralysing grains, I was in intense pain for days, as though every single muscle had been overworked, and I could only sip drinks and soup as my throat was so sore. Luckily, my mum looked after me. She was always kind when we were sick...though neither she nor my father enquired further into what had actually happened.

My Practitioner had me notice what I was feeling in my body. My mind was telling me I was 'wasting my session' with this random story but she suggested staying with it a little longer. I started to have a very strange but familiar feeling creep around the back of my skull.

It wasn't the 'whooshing' out the back of dissociation but, instead, kind of like a blankety helmet enveloping my head with pain in the base of my skull. It was becoming very hard to form words and I felt I was looking at my Practitioner through very hooded eyes.

I was reminded of other things going on around the time of this dental surgery experience. I was on epilepsy drugs and spent many days in my teacher training lecture theatre, with its low banks of fluorescent lights, fighting off these similar feelings, seeing a white 'aura' appear around the lecturer, and now it was there, around my Practitioner.

I felt my body start to 'give in' to the 'seizure', felt my jaw start to tense, and my forearm, so we dialled it back a bit. I was amazed that I was able to still be there with it but not going to that old familiar place of fighting off the clenching and then giving in to it and eventually 'passing out' (I could always hear though, as far as I could tell, so used to think I was 'doing it for attention' somehow).

My Practitioner, at one point, had me count backwards from ten, the way I did with the anaesthesia. I could only get to nine and started to shake and cry. My head felt very, very strange, like in a fog. Her take on it was I was 'in the anaesthesia', that I had had a near death experience and this was the survival energy AND the anaesthetic stuck in my body...and we were helping it move out!!

I think I had a big release, possibly with tears and trembling; I'm a little unclear on that point. But I slowly felt myself returning to 'normal transmission', until I was laughing and 'fine'. I had a HUGE realisation that the anaesthetist had SAVED MY LIFE (and so did my blue fingernails). I'd never had it mirrored anywhere that I'd been in a life and death situation. But when I looked things up afterward, yes, blue fingernails were a sign of either cardiac or respiratory failure.

This whole experience definitely created greater capacity in my nervous system because the very next day, I had to go and have a tooth removed and I handled it like a BOSS! I stopped them when I needed to and trembled and cried AND I was able to self-soothe through the pain and the triggering trauma of them doing painful things in my mouth, even though I hadn't been able to bring outside support with me. I didn't need to use pain killers of any kind...and it was a big tooth!

Soon after that, I attended a meditation class and it became clear that when I put my attention on breathing, and especially the experience of emptying the lungs and briefly being in that space of 'no breath', panic would usually surface right at that point...which must be VERY reminiscent to my body of 'respiratory failure': of literally having no breath inside me and not being able to get any!

It all made so much sense - the years of panic attacks brought on by elevated heart rate, the difficulty in meditation every time my focus is on the breath - my body is triggered. Even though my mind was unconscious, my body remembers.

And, bless its cotton socks, my body has been trying to heal on that all these years, taking me to the place, over and over, where it can attempt to offload the 'inability to breath' and the survival energy stuck there...and my mind has sensed the panicked feelings and freaked out, doing all it can to pull me out of that dangerous situation. My darling body. At the end of that session with my Practitioner, I actually FELT how miraculous my body is: how SENTIENT, how IN MY BEST INTERESTS it is. And I feel excited, once again, about life.

I have since had another session with the same Practitioner dedicated to clearing more, where my body released the stored energy in a very gentle way. And I am happy to say that I can now walk my dog around the block without going into a 'hard-to-breathe' meltdown. Other situations where my heart rate rises, like being in social settings, I now only have what I think of as common, garden-variety anxiety, not what feels like life-threatening panic. I'm so grateful.

*With still so little recognition within mainstream Western medicine of the connection between our physiological and psychological experiences, we have a long way to go before necessary changes take place. It's through bringing conversations like Wendy's into our conscious awareness that acknowledgement can grow and influence research to bring about that shift.*

# Melanie is Kinda Proud of her NOTE transformation!

*Melanie Morfitt from Winnipeg, Manitoba, Canada #Emerges Proud to tell us how 'Nothing is sacred to the tornado of change whose mission it is to destroy all things not aligned with truth'. That is the transformative power of NOTES...*

> "For a seed to achieve its greatest expression, it must come completely undone. The shell cracks, its insides come out and everything changes. To someone who doesn't understand growth, it would look like complete destruction."
> Cynthia Occelli

## Suddenly Awake

As I grabbed my mittens and scurried out into the cold January evening, I was unaware that my soul was totally in charge that night. My "perfect" life had led me into a dark depression, and now the internal pleas for help were leading me to a workshop at my local library in Aurora, Ontario, Canada.

"YOU MUST PLACE YOURSELF FIRST", had appeared on the tearstained page I was journaling upon just days earlier. As a mother of two active preschoolers, who juggled single-parenting most of the time while my husband traveled, placing myself first was a foreign concept to me in 1996.

It had been several years now since I had used writing as a balm to soothe the pain of my childhood. Six long years of wearing full body casts from chin bone to tailbone 24/7 had begun when I was ten years old, and had honed my skills well as a victim of childhood idiopathic scoliosis. Years of plaster and plastic, and doctors' appointments, had left many scars on me, although most of them were invisible.

A few days before, as I had stared at those five words of wisdom demanding attention, a fresh crack appeared in my shell. I immediately walked to the front door of my perfect two-storey brick suburban home, retrieved the newspaper from my mailbox, and circled an ad that felt like destiny had called. A free seminar at my local library promised it could bring relaxation and healing to the body. Great! I could use some loosening up.

The night of the presentation, thirty fellow spectators were sitting spellbound as we listened and watched volunteers receive samples of a particular bodywork. Recipients were delighted by the small but obvious changes they experienced as the middle-aged gentle man with the Egyptian accent at the front of the room worked on their bodies. The innate wisdom and ability of the body to heal itself wasn't a new concept to me; however, this method of reminding the body through a particular manipulation technique certainly was.

"Who has back pain issues?" was the presenter's next question. As my hand shot up, our eyes locked, and I excitedly accepted my turn for healing. I positioned myself face down on the small wooden massage table, draped with a simple white sheet, and awaited my relief. After perhaps 10 or 15 minutes of demonstration, I realized that I had slipped into a very welcomed, relaxed state of being. "Hey Mel…are ya still here?" I heard my friend Tracey shout from the audience. "Yes, I'm fine," I exclaimed back in reassurance. I then heard the bodywork practitioner softly request, "Now before you get off the table, I'd like you to slowly pull yourself up into a foetal position so I can sneak a bit of work directly on your back". I obediently curled up into a child's pose and felt a warm palm being applied to my spine, serendipitously directly above the scar on my back where I had been sliced open 18 years previously as a 15-year-old child.

WHAM! I was instantly gone! I was out-of-body, suddenly experiencing the precise moment that my orthopaedic surgeon was about to use his scalpel to pierce my skin to begin 4 ½ hours of surgery to my spine. It was now September 1978, not a memory, but I exist there right now in real time. "STOP!" I attempted to scream out. But, as I hovered out-of-body about eight feet above my 15-year-old self in 1978, I helplessly realized that, as pure consciousness in that moment, I had no voice. The emotional intensity of the reality brought my awareness back to the massage table in the library in 1996. I heard the calm voice of the practitioner intuitively redirect me, "Just stay with it", and, once again, without warning, I was whisked BACK out-of-body, and deposited back at the same 1978 scene.

I instantly realized that although I had returned to the same horror-filled moment of confusion, I was simultaneously wrapped with a download of understanding and knowingness that existed beyond all thought. I felt the winds of truth fanning the embers within my cells into full flames that ripped through my internal neighborhoods of fear and ignorance. Nothing is sacred to the tornado of change whose mission it is to destroy all things not aligned with truth. As I existed here out-of-body in this place beyond time, I simply knew things with perfect clarity. I understood my entire childhood and the choices and actions and inactions that led me to that moment of hopelessness in the operating room. I KNEW things without questions cloaking their light. I had never been a victim.

And, just as quickly as this experience began, I felt myself collapse back into a body that existed in a library in a moment that was January 16th 1996. Primal instincts instructed my lungs to breathe as I was suddenly aware of audible sobbing, coming from a depth of pain and overload of new wisdom that simply could not fit back into this small human frame.

The moment was perfection, and yet it was complete destruction. I just experienced myself as pure consciousness without a body, in a place more real than the one I had just returned to.

I inhaled my first breath as an awakened being, faintly detecting the acrid odor of internal maps and atheist beliefs all around me smoldering from love's perfect strike. As I eventually got up to leave my chrysalis at the front of the room, a single thought wafted like wind beneath my wet wings, "EVERYTHING HAPPENS FOR A REASON", and I instantly knew that I was suddenly AWAKE.

It was after that night of transformation that my healing and awakening journey truly began. I suddenly had no fear of death whatsoever. The reality I had experienced was MORE REAL than the one that

I had returned to. My cells now knew that "everything happens for a reason", which led to a rearrangement of my perspectives from victim into student. Finding myself dropped onto the opposite shores of reality as a spiritual being instead of an atheist was confusing to the mind but has remained permanent. And what was this term I had never even heard of before now pulsing in my veins, "AWAKE?" The knowingness was instant and undeniable: I am a spiritual being having a human experience, and not the other way around.

Truly remarkable were not just the inner changes that took place, but the physical "evidence" of my shift. For several months light-bulbs would burn out instantly around me, and electrical devices would malfunction. Inspired writing would wake me up at all hours of the night, and a thirst beyond all thirsts for reading material of the body/mind connection and metaphysical worlds was incessant (a small challenge in 1996, as the internet was not yet at my disposal for research). Memories of past lives and dreams shared with my young daughter and lucid dreaming were now firsts for me, as were so many other new wonders that made it so magical to finally feel truly alive and wide awake!

We are all on this journey of awakening from the unconscious dream, beginning to remember who we truly are. We are infinite, intelligent energy - ever expanding and experiencing more in a cosmos that uses LOVE to create. Simple really...

*Simple, beautiful, and yet so very challenging. After*

*we've had such an awakening, navigating the world 'in human form' can be so very painful, and why it's so vital to connect with others who understand.*

# Magdalena has used her personal turmoil as a 'wake-up' compass to direct her life purpose

*As most of us discover after years of trying to make a difference in the world - by being busy 'doing' good - Magdalena Smieszek found that it was her journey within that really gifted her the insight of her personal quest in connection to the whole of humanity. Her personal agony acted as a 'wake-up call' for healing both individually and collectively. As Magdalena explains, it was her birthright as a human to experience a profound spiritually transformative experience, and one that is now helping her to integrate more fully with her life purpose...*

# The Human Quest for Meaning

Our individual stories are connected in intricate ways to our collective stories. Like all stories, mine has had twists and turns, but the one thing that has been consistent is my search for meaning. Throughout life, I was especially drawn to the theme of justice. Influenced by my migratory and refugee childhood, the plight of the outsider, in whatever form, tore at my heartstrings. This embedded sense about injustice led to a career as a human rights advocate and humanitarian, hopeful that I too, in Gandhi style wisdom, can realize the change I want in the world. In fact, this objective took me round and round the world to do my little part in alleviating suffering. That to me was the right thing to do, the most meaningful thing. Giving and receiving should equalize, I always thought. That's a reasonable view, but also contentious as to where and how we attribute value.

Then came a time in my mid-thirties where the accumulated connection to the suffering of others had compounded my own suffering. I started to lose hope. The extent of human misery was overwhelming. I felt helpless when reflecting on the seemingly endless road of hurt that human beings inflict on each other. Distraught at the predicament of humanity as a whole - all the conflicts around the globe, and my own identity crisis in thinking that, despite my best efforts, I'm unable to do anything about it - I was thrust into despair. After years of connecting with many people and places, I disconnected from the outside world. I had gone far and wide to explore the external reality, and finally here I was, turning back to the point of origin, turning inside for much needed inner work and exploration.

I went into a deep meditative and transcendent state in which a powerful energetic force took over and pulled me through the doors of perception. On the other side was something incredibly profound – a tour of my own unconscious inner world and, even further, an exploration of the collective unconscious. So much of it is beautiful, for volumes to be filled. Just as much of it is dreadful, and yet we must confront it. Whatever doubt of the divine that I held, it dissolved. To me there was no mistaking it, I had a spiritual awakening of the most profound kind, the kind on which prophecies, spiritual traditions, and sacred texts are based. These days it can be shameful to say something like that. Who am I to say I had a visionary revelation, a Buddha-like enlightenment, a shamanic initiation, an awakening of such perfection and insight as Christ consciousness? Well, I am not ashamed to say – I am a human being, hence this is my birthright, and it happened.

In various degrees it lasted for days, weeks, and years, and it is still doing its work. This wasn't a one-time occurrence but an opening and a process, sometimes blissful and sometimes distressing. The most meaningful part has been connecting my very personal experience to consensus reality – that process of integration; because as long as we live, it is not just in this miraculous inner universe but in a shared truth, even if this truth is continually shifting. I can get immersed in my inner experience, but the point is to bring it back, learn from it, expand, transform, connect, evolve, and create more beauty. Not only did I have a renewed hope, sense of purpose, and a vision, but a new index of downloaded information that I had to sort through.

How to bring it back and connect has been revealing itself as I move forward in life. In some ways it's obvious because human rights, aka the topic I've been obsessed with most of my life, are the evolving wisdom about human treatment drawn from numerous sources over generations and that includes spiritual traditions. But it goes back even further. An aspect of what we now call human rights have been in our unconscious before they took the form of conscious creations. They are tools for healing. This is our evolving universal morality for our betterment as individuals in our own unique story, and as humanity in our continually expanding collective story, transforming from immense pain and suffering towards greater compassion, care, inclusion, and love. We're doing this by recognition of our shared dignity, our sacredness, our increasing empathy, and our expanding consciousness about what it means to be human as we include more and more experiences into our domain of understanding. This means also confronting the shadowy expressions of our existence.

Clearly there's more work to do. There's no shortage of pain and suffering in the world. That agony is a wake-up call for both individual and collective healing. Throughout history, mystics of all sorts have sought to create conditions for peace and love among humankind: not perfectly I may say, but in a very human way. They took the extraordinary turmoil of their awakening experience to create knowledge, movements, shifts in consciousness, and we are living their achievements. Now it's our turn. How's that for meaningful?

*We couldn't agree more Magdalena, what really seems to be at the core of our search for meaning is to collectively make the world a better place to live. As Roald Dahl says;*

*"Inside all of us is the power to change the world"*

# Resources for NOTE-ers

International Spiritual Emergence Networks:
http://www.spiritualemergencenetwork.org/find-networks/

UK Spiritual Crisis Network:
http://spiritualcrisisnetwork.uk
Email for support: spiritualcrisis@gmail.com

IANDS (International Association for Near Death Studies): https://iands.org

ACISTE (American Centre for the Integration of Spiritually Transformative Experiences):
https://aciste.org

IMHU (Integrative Mental Health for You):
https://imhu.org

## Online forums

Shades of Awakening:
http://shadesofawakening.com (Facebook group)

Spirit Release:
http://www.spiritrelease.org

## Peer Support Groups

UK:
https://spiritualcrisisnetwork.uk/help/peer-support-groups/ or
https://emergingproud.com/tek-peer-groups/

The Death Cafe:
https://deathcafe.com

ONLINE:
https://isgo.iands.org or

http://spiritualemergenceanonymous.org/meetings/

For a private therapist or / information and other resources: https://aworldawake.org

## Aligned Support Organisations

Hearing Voices Network:
https://www.hearing-voices.org
Email: info@hearing-voices.org

Mad in America: https://www.madinamerica.com

A Disorder for Everyone:
http://www.adisorder4everyone.com

Compassionate Mental Health:
http://compassionatementalhealth.co.uk

Inner Compass: moving away from diagnosis /
coming off medication support:
https://www.theinnercompass.org

Holotropic Breathwork:
www.holotropicuk.co.uk / www.holotropic.com

MAPS (Multidisciplinary Association for Psychedelic
Studies): https://maps.org

Kundalini specific information:
http://kundalinicare.com /
http://www.kundaliniguide.com

### Retreats and Safe Spaces

Safely Held Spaces: https://www.safelyheldspaces.org

Wales, UK: http://www.dolifor-centre.com Email:
retreats@innerlife.org.uk or telephone: 01597 810168

US: North Carolina; Centre for Spiritual Emergence:
http://www.centerforspiritualemergence.com

San Francisco; Gnosis Centre
http://www.gnosisretreatcenter.org

California; Esalen: https://www.esalen.org

LA; Pine manor: http://pinemanor.com

# Helpful Reading / Viewing
# recommended by NOTE-ers*

## Books

The Power of NOTEs, Dr Nicole Gruel
Mend the Gap, Katie Mottram
In Case of Spiritual Emergency, Catherine G Lucas
Farther Shores, Yvonne Kason MD
Breaking Down is Waking Up, Dr Russell Razzaque
Out of the Darkness: From Turmoil to Transformation,
Steve Taylor
The Leap, Steve Taylor
Ask, Believe, Receive, Abraham Hicks
You can Heal Your Life, Louise Hay
A New Earth, Eckhart Tolle
A Return to Love, Marianne Williamson

## Books continued

The Call of Spiritual Emergency, Emma Bragdon
Spiritual Crisis: Varieties and perspectives of a
transpersonal phenomenon, Fransje de Waard
Spiritual Emergency: When personal transformation
becomes a crisis, Stanislav Grof
The kundalini guide, Bonnie Greenwell
The awakening guide, Bonnie Greenwell
The Stormy Search for the Self, Stanislav Grof
Psychosis and Spirituality; Consolidating the new
Paradigm, Isabel Clarke
The Red Book, Carl Jung
Trials of the Visionary Mind; Spiritual Emergency and
the Renewal Process, John W. Perry

The Far Side of madness, John W. Perry

What is Self? A study of the spiritual journey in terms of consciousness, Bernadette Roberts

Healing the Split; Integrating Spirit Into our understanding of the mentally ill, John E Nelson

Journey Through Transformation: A guide to mystical awakening, kundalini, emotional clearing and spiritual emergence, Kaia Nightingale

Spiritual Psychiatries, Natalie Tobert

Cultural Perspectives on Mental Wellbeing: Spiritual Interpretations of Symptoms in Medical Practice, Natalie Tobert

Unshrinking Psychosis, Understanding and Healing the Wounded Soul, John Watkins

Varieties of religious experience, William James

Rethinking Madness, Paris Williams

After the Ecstasy the Laundry, Jack Kornfield

Breaking Down is Waking Up, Russell Razzaque

Madness, mystery and the survival of God, Isabel Clarke

Psychosis and Spirituality, Isabel Clarke

Introduction to Religious and Spiritual Experiences, Rankin

The Hero's Journey, Joseph Campbell

The Power of Now, Eckhart Tolle

Conversations with God, Neale Donald Walsch

The Celestine Prophecy, James Redfield

Developing Consciousness, Nicholas Vesey

Synchro-Destiny, Deepak Chopra

Divine Intervention, Dawn Chrystal

Seth Material, Jane Roberts

Untethered Soul, Michael Singer

Abraham Hicks Books, Esther and Jerry Hicks

The Transformative Power of Near-Death Experiences,
Dr Penny Sartori and Kelly Walsh
The Unselfish Spirit and The Visionary Spirit, Dr Mick
Collins

## Films

CRAZYWISE documentary
#Emerging Proud film
Healing Voices
The Secret
The Celestine Prophecy
What the Bleep do we know?
The Shift

## Podcasts / videos

Under the Skin, Podcast by Russell Brand
Waking up Bipolar, Podcast by Chris Cole
Teal Swan teachings, You Tube
Am I bipolar or waking up? Sean Blackwell, You Tube
series

*The resources in the above lists are taken from
those indicated as helpful by the #Emerging Proud
community when consulted specifically for this
project. They are examples, and by no means meant as
an exhaustive list.

# Self Care Tips

## ISEN's Crisis Guide; *Emerge Out of your Crisis*

A crisis is different for everyone, but one thing is the same for all of us; when we are in crisis we can feel as though everything is falling apart.

To see your crisis as part of a 'breakdown to breakthrough' process can help to give a sense of hope.

This guide aims to give you some simple but vital tools that can help you to stay safe and manage your process to 'emerge' out of your crisis.

Having our experiences validated as 'normal', real, natural and meaningful can be one of the most important aspects of being able to heal and grow.

It's vital that we are kind to ourselves during this time, and allow any emotions to surface and be expressed in a safe environment.

Having peer support from someone who has gone through similar experiences, and can listen without judgement, is really helpful. Go to the back page to find the resources that will be most helpful for you in your local area.

You are not alone! What you are going through is a normal part of a healing process. Don't give up – there is light at the end of the tunnel even when you feel in complete darkness.

You are not crazy, you are becoming well and growing into wholeness, and that is a painful process.

## Quick Tips

1. Allow your vulnerability – it's a strength…allow your tears to fall and your heart to shine – it's the best way we can connect as humans and feel less alone.

2. Allow yourself to 'turn up whole' and trust that it's all part of the process. This also means acknowledging that it's okay to have 'dark' thoughts and uncomfortable emotions

3. Breathe - It's normal to feel that you have no stability when you are going through such a process of immense change, but it will settle down and get easier to manage

4. Find a safe environment e.g. with a therapist or in a group, to help you work through trauma when it arises to be healed. Releasing your emotions; verbally, physically and in any other way necessary is vital

5. Focus on your self care - Getting physical exercise / being in nature / eating wholesome food and getting plenty of sleep is important. Initially, some prescribed medications may be necessary to help you manage your life

6. Avoid stimulants (alcohol / drugs / caffeine /

processed foods, especially sugar)

7. Join a support group – this can be an online forum / it helps not to isolate yourself. Try to find at least one person you trust where you can openly talk about your experiences without fear of being judged

8. Reduce stress wherever possible; both at home and work

9. Reduce spiritual practices, as this can make your experience more intense

10. Listen to calming or uplifting music, and also listening to the sounds of nature can be helpful

11. Relationships - spend time with supportive people, and distance yourself from ones that feel stressful

12. Creative self-expression is helpful when you find talking difficult, e.g. drawing, painting, poetry, music, drumming, sculpture, singing

13. If you are already taking prescribed medication, it is not advisable to reduce or stop this without clinical guidance

### Food

Remembering to eat really helps. You may find that at different stages of your process you might be drawn to, and need, different types of food.

The general consensus seems to be that heavier foods are useful for grounding, these include grains, root vegetables, pulses, dairy products and meat. Protein should be an important element in your diet although, at times, animal products may become difficult to digest; in this case, to switch to plant-related protein sources e.g. pulses or grain can be a better choice for your well-being.

Be aware that sweet foods and sugar can affect blood sugar levels, which can in turn destabilise your mood. Avoid stimulants such as caffeine, which is found in coffee, but also tea, fizzy drinks and in chocolate. Alcohol and fat-laden processed foods, with no nutritional content, can make you feel sluggish.

It's important to eat fresh food any time you can, drink a lot, mainly water. Eat less, more often, is the healthiest way to manage your diet. However, fasting can intensify your experience.

Vitamins and minerals are vital for your balance, e.g. vitamins C, vitamin B, Iron and Calcium.
You may be able to tune into your physical well-being and listen to what your body is calling for rather than what your mind is saying you 'should' be eating. Our bodies have a wisdom of their own if we can learn to listen to it.

### Sleep

Normal sleep patterns can be interrupted, which may be OK for a short time, especially if it's possible to rest as and when it's needed. However, prolonged loss of sleep can make your experience more difficult to cope with, so you could try some simple relaxation methods such as - taking a bubble bath, doing some relaxation breathing techniques, listening to guided meditations, using Lavender oil and drinking chamomile tea.

If you are feeling anxious or frightened, herbal remedies can help. If possible, ask a practitioner for advice on something to suit your needs. If herbs don't help, consider seeking medical advice; taking a sleeping tablet for a few nights may help re-establish a normal sleep pattern.

## Nature

Try to spend lots of time in nature.

It may sound simple or obvious but spending time in the natural environment can really help a great deal. For people experiencing psychological distress, focusing on the calmness of nature can give a sense of grounding and relief from the confusion happening in the mind.

Perhaps there is something in the following list that you can do –

- Do some gardening (or even offer to help in a neighbour's garden) - plant some flowers in a window box or indoors; grow some veggies
- Go for a walk in the woods
- Get involved with a group that works out in nature or helps clean up the local environment. This can be a great way to meet other people and make friends too.
- Allow yourself to get dirty - Having fun and getting in touch with the earth can be healing.

## Exercise

Some people find vigorous exercise like running, very helpful because of the increased amount of energy they are experiencing in their bodies. Others find gentle walking or yoga to be more what they need. Creative exercise e.g. Dancing, Drumming or even Hula-hooping can help to release some energy from your body. Let your body move in whatever ways feel natural to you...

## Spiritual Practices

At the beginning of a crisis it's advisable to stop or at least reduce any spiritual practices, e.g. meditation, to slow down your process; these can then be gradually re-introduced over time.

## Stress

It's very common to experience high levels of anxiety during these times. This can present as shallow breathing, palpitations, sweating, confusion or even panic attacks. There are some simple and effective self- help tools that can help you manage these, like a guided body scan, e.g. the Autogenic Technique. Remember also the basic tips on relaxation included in the sleep section, and the benefits gained from releasing emotions and talking openly to someone you trust.

## Creativity and Self Expression

Many people find times of crisis to also be a time when their creative energies are active. Painting, drawing, craftwork; these can be used as a way of expressing experiences, releasing emotions and bringing a sense of focus. Enjoy the creation of whatever comes, rather than focusing on the final outcome; messy is good!

Dancing, movement, singing and playing music, can create an enormous release of energy. Even when having a bad day, listening to your favourite music and dancing around has an enormous power of positive refocusing. Turn the music up loud and let out those pent-up screams too; it can be very cathartic to release repressed emotions.

Simple things like writing stories, poetry, upcycling old furniture or clothing, changing your bedroom around, all help with creative expression.

Go slow - Small steps can have a big impact, especially when they lead to a growing sense of satisfaction and confidence.

## Suicidal thoughts and Self Harm

Even though a crisis can be growth towards healing, there may be times when it is extremely dark, terrifying, and dangerous; it is common to experience having suicidal thoughts and thoughts of self-harm.

There are, however, a lot of things that can help manage this distress, more of which can be found on this link: https://www.metanoia.org/suicide/.

The fact is you are not alone — other people have felt deep and terrible pain and come through it - you can too.

1. Feeling suicidal does not have to mean giving up on life.

If you are feeling suicidal it may be that you are desperate for things to be different. Wanting this life to end doesn't rule out the possibility of a new, better life beginning, but you may feel like that is beyond reach right now. Imagine what a better life might look like and see how it is possible to realise it if you stick around to find out what could happen. Turn some of that suicidal energy towards risking change in your life. Consider that it may be a behaviour pattern or life condition that you want to end. Ask yourself, "What inside me needs to die?".

2. Feeling suicidal often leads to isolation

It's vital that you find someone to talk with confidentially on a deep level, someone who is not going to judge or reject what you say. There is no need to feel ashamed of whatever you are feeling. Admitting our vulnerabilities can be terrifying, but once we open up it can bring a huge sense of relief. Sharing any plans with just one person can help to keep you safe.

**Tips to keep yourself safe**

- Remember that your thoughts do not have to take charge; you can have them without acting on them
- If you are feeling like hurting yourself; wait, even if it's for 5 mins, but just wait, and breathe... this may be hard but it's likely the intensity will subside
- Call a person or group you can trust to open up to about how you feel
- Find a safe way to express any emotions that are surfacing
- Call a helpline

*"So whatever turmoil or turbulence life presents to you, know that it has happened for a reason; you broke down so that you may wake up. You got lost so that you may find yourself again."*

**Dr Russell Razzaque**

**Breaking Down Is Waking Up**

# Acknowledgements

My infinite thanks go to the incredible KindaProud team; the book Reps, and especially Dr Nicole Gruel for spearheading, and Mandy Horne for editing, this particular edition in the series. Our Publisher Sean Patrick of That Guy's House and PR Consultant Jenna Owen of Media Jems, all of whom have passionately and without question donated their time and expertise in order to support this project to fruition. It's a vision we all share, and one that would not have been possible to achieve without each and every one of us coming together with no agenda other than wanting to disseminate hope like confetti around the world…

The team also extends our immense gratitude to everyone in this pocket book, who have bravely gifted their personal transformation story with the hope that it helps at least one other person in the world to find their own inner spark to initiate or aid their recovery journey. We aim for these books to create a 'positive domino effect', rippling out HOPE to those who need it most.

Our gratitude also goes to The Missing Kind charity who seed-funded this project as an official Sponsor, and ISEN (the International Spiritual Emergence Network) for allowing us to use their crisis guide as a resource.

Without all of these team players there would be no HOPE confetti, so together we celebrate the incredible power of heart-founded collaboration, and a shared vision and mission.

The KindaProud Team

Other titles in our KindaProud Pocket Books of Hope and Transformation series so far

#Emerging Proud through Disordered Eating, Body Image and Low Self-Esteem

#Emerging Proud through Suicide

#Emerging Proud through Trauma and Abuse

Hope

It's all I need
to lift my heart
out of the depths
and into the light

By Ambriel